Pagan Portals
&
Shaman Pathways

...an ever-growing library of shared knowledge.

Moon Books has created two unique series where leading authors and practitioners come together to share their knowledge, passion and expertise across the complete Pagan spectrum. If you would like to contribute to either series, our proposal procedure is simple and quick, just visit our website (www.MoonBooks.net) and click on Author Inquiry to begin the process.

If you are a reader with a comment about a book or a suggestion for a title we'd love to hear from you! You can find us at facebook.com/MoonBooks or you can keep up to date with new releases etc on our dedicated Portals page at facebook.com/paganportalsandshamanpathways/

'Moon Books has achieved that rare feat of being synonymous with top-quality authorship AND being endlessly innovative and exciting.'
Kate Large, Pagan Dawn

Pagan Portals

Animal Magic, Rachel Patterson
An introduction to the world of animal magic and working with animal spirit guides

Australian Druidry, Julie Brett
Connect with the magic of the southern land, its seasons, animals, plants and spirits

Blacksmith Gods, Pete Jennings
Exploring dark folk tales and customs alongside the magic and myths of the blacksmith Gods through time and place

Brigid, Morgan Daimler
Meeting the Celtic Goddess of Poetry, Forge, and Healing Well

By Spellbook & Candle, Mélusine Draco
Why go to the bother of cursing, when a bottling or binding can be just as effective?

By Wolfsbane & Mandrake Root, Mélusine Draco
A study of poisonous plants, many of which have beneficial uses in both domestic medicine and magic

Candle Magic, Lucya Starza
Using candles in simple spells, seasonal rituals and essential craft techniques

Celtic Witchcraft, Mabh Savage
Wield winds of wyrd, dive into pools of wisdom; walk side by side with the Tuatha Dé Danann

Dancing with Nemetona, Joanna van der Hoeven
An in-depth look at a little-known Goddess who can help bring peace and sanctuary into your life

Fairy Witchcraft, Morgan Daimler
A guidebook for those seeking a path that combines modern Neopagan witchcraft with the older Celtic Fairy Faith

God-Speaking, Judith O'Grady
What can we do to save the planet? Three Rs are not enough. Reduce, reuse, recycle...and religion

Gods and Goddesses of Ireland,
Meet the Gods and Goddesses of Pagan Ireland in myth and modern practice

Grimalkyn: The Witch's Cat, Martha Gray
A mystical insight into the cat as a power animal

Hedge Riding, Harmonia Saille
The hedge is the symbolic boundary between the two worlds and this book will teach you how to cross that hedge

Hedge Witchcraft, Harmonia Saille
Learning by experiencing is about trusting your instincts and connecting with your inner spirit

Hekate, Vivienne Moss
The Goddess of Witches, Queen of Shades and Shadows, and the ever-eternal Dark Muse haunts the pages of this poetic devotional, enchanting those who love Her with the charm only this Dark Goddess can bring

Herbs of the Sun, Moon and Planets, Steve Andrews
The planets that rule over herbs that grow on Earth

Hoodoo, Rachel Patterson
Learn about and experience the fascinating magical art of Hoodoo

Irish Paganism, Morgan Daimler
Reconstructing the beliefs and practices of pre-Christian Irish Paganism for the modern world

Kitchen Witchcraft, Rachel Patterson
Take a glimpse at the workings of a Kitchen Witch and share in the crafts

Meditation, Rachel Patterson
An introduction to the beautiful world of meditation

Merlin: Once and Future Wizard, Elen Sentier
Merlin in history, Merlin in mythology, Merlin through the ages and his continuing relevance

Moon Magic, Rachel Patterson
An introduction to working with the phases of the Moon

Nature Mystics, Rebecca Beattie
Tracing the literary origins of modern Paganism

Pan, Mélusine Draco
An historical, mythological and magical insight into the God Pan

Pathworking through Poetry, Fiona Tinker
Discover the esoteric knowledge in the works of Yeats, O'Sullivan and other poets

Runes, Kylie Holmes

The Runes are a set of 24 symbols that are steeped in history, myths and legends. This book offers practical and accessible information for anyone to understand this ancient form of divination

Sacred Sex and Magick, Web PATH Center

Wrap up ecstasy in love to create powerful magick, spells and healing

Spirituality without Structure, Nimue Brown

The only meaningful spiritual journey is the one you consciously undertake

The Awen Alone, Joanna van der Hoeven

An introductory guide for the solitary Druid

The Cailleach, Rachel Patterson

Goddess of the ancestors, wisdom that comes with age, the weather, time, shape-shifting and winter

The Morrigan, Morgan Daimler

On shadowed wings and in raven's call, meet the ancient Irish Goddess of war, battle, prophecy, death, sovereignty, and magic

Urban Ovate, Brendan Howlin

Simple, accessible techniques to bring Druidry to the wider public

Your Faery Magic, Halo Quin

Tap into your Natural Magic and become the Fey you are

Zen Druidry, Joanna van der Hoeven
Zen teachings and Druidry combine to create a peaceful life
path that is completely dedicated to the here and now

Shaman Pathways

Aubry's Dog, Melusine Draco
A practical and essential guide to using canine magical energies

Black Horse White Horse, Mélusine Draco
Feel the power and freedom as Black Horse, White Horse
guides you down the magical path of this most noble animal

Celtic Chakras, Elen Sentier
Tread the British native shaman's path, explore the Goddess
hidden in the ancient stories; walk the Celtic chakra spiral
labyrinth

Druid Shaman, Danu Forest
A practical guide to Celtic shamanism with exercises and
techniques as well as traditional lore for exploring the Celtic
Otherworld

Elen of the Ways, Elen Sentier
British shamanism has largely been forgotten: the reindeer
Goddess of the ancient Boreal forest is shrouded in mystery...
follow her deer-trods to rediscover her old ways

Following the Deer Trods, Elen Sentier
A practical handbook for anyone wanting to begin the old
British paths. Follows on from Elen of the Ways

Trees of the Goddess, Elen Sentier
Work with the trees of the Goddess and the old ways of Britain

Way of the Faery Shaman, Flavia Kate Peters
Your practical insight into Faeries and the elements they engage
to unlock real magic that is waiting to help you

Web of Life, Yvonne Ryves
A new approach to using ancient ways in these contemporary
and often challenging times to weave your life path

Pagan Portals

Divination:

By Rod, Fingers & Birds

A companion volume to *By Spellbook & Candle* and *By Wolfsbane & Mandrake Root*

Pagan Portals
Divination:
By Rod, Fingers & Birds

A companion volume to *By Spellbook &
Candle* and *By Wolfsbane & Mandrake Root*

Mélusine Draco

Winchester, UK
Washington, USA

First published by Moon Books, 2018
Moon Books is an imprint of John Hunt Publishing Ltd., No. 3 East St., Alresford,
Hampshire SO24 9EE, UK
office1@jhpbooks.net
www.johnhuntpublishing.com
www.moon-books.net

For distributor details and how to order please visit the 'Ordering' section on our website.

Design: Stuart Davies

Printed and bound by CPI Group (UK) Ltd, Croydon, CR0 4YY, UK

We operate a distinctive and ethical publishing philosophy in
all areas of our business, from our global network of authors to
production and worldwide distribution.

Contents

For Adrien … for asking the questions

Chapter One

The Practical Approach

It was Robert Cochrane who originally coined those now famous words:

> *If one who claims to be a Witch can perform the tasks of Witchcraft, i.e. summon the spirits and they come,* **can divine with rod, fingers and birds***. If they can also claim the right to the omens and have them; have the power to call, heal and curse and above all, can tell the maze and cross the Lethe, then you have a witch.*

Divination is what I would refer to as the practical element of Craft magic, and we don't even have to be witches to be able to read the portents. But it helps!

Looking into the future is a very ancient practice. As we saw in the chapter: Developing the 'Art of Seeing', in *Traditional Witchcraft for Urban Living*, thousands of recorded British customs and superstitions all have their roots in fortune-telling spells and charms, and they are as fashionable today as they were way back when. In fact, it's been said that divination was as commonplace in the past as satellite communication is today: it was part of everyday life for everyone from king to commoner. It utilised all manner of techniques and methods from a simple nut placed on the fire grate to the complicated reading of the Roman auspices.

For example a few of these techniques include:

Aeromancy: Divination using the formation of clouds and other patterns in the skies.

Botanomancy: Divination through plant life; may include the burning of plants and foretelling future events through the ashes or smoke.

Crystallomancy: An ancient form of casting lots using small stones. Or **crystalomancy:** Divination by studying a crystal ball.

Daphnomancy: Using the smoke of burning branches of the laurel tree to answer questions and forecast upcoming events.

Enoptromancy: An ancient method using a shiny surface placed in water.

Felidomancy: Divination through the observation of felines, including domestic and wild cats.

Geomancy: An ancient system interpreting the patterns and shapes or events found in nature.

Halomancy: Foretelling by interpreting the formation of the crystals when salt is poured to the ground.

Ichthyomancy: Observing the behaviour of fish both in and out of the water.

Jungism: The understanding of mythic symbolism as it relates to the human subconscious.

Kephalonomancy: Ancient method of pouring lighted carbon on the skull of a goat or donkey to determine guilt or innocence.

Lampadomancy: Divination through the observation of flames from a candle or flaming torch.

Metopomancy: Divination and character analysis by studying the lines on a person's forehead.

Necromancy: Contacting the spirits of the dead to interpret omens and forecast future events.

Oinomancy: An ancient Roman practice of interpretation through the study and evaluation of the colour, consistency and taste of wine.

Psephomancy: Divination by selecting at random, small stones from a pile.

Qabbala: A blend of powerful divinely-inspired divination and mysticism.

Rune Stones: A series of mystic symbols thrown or selected to determine the future.

Scrying: Divination by interpreting the play of light on a shiny object or surface.

Tephramancy: Interpreting the ashes of a combustible object.

Uromancy: Divination using urine.

Visualisation: A controlled level of consciousness during which the seeker can divine answers to questions.

Wort-Lore: The understanding of the appropriate herbs to use to aid divination.

Xylomancy: Using the arrangement of dried sticks to predict the future.

Ying-Yang: Describe how seemingly opposite or contrary forces may actually be complementary, interconnected, and interdependent in the natural world, and how they may interrelate to one another and influence future events.

Zoanthropy: Divination by observing and interpreting the flames of three lighted candles placed in a triangular position.

A deep-rooted belief in divination has existed throughout the ages, among both the uncivilized and the most civilized of cultures, as the desire to know the future continually gave rise to some weird and wonderful ways of peering into it. The Egyptians used dreams (i.e. temple sleep) to divine the will of the gods; the Druids used many different forms of divination, as did the Hebrews. Although augury was first implemented by the Chaldeans, the Greeks became addicted to it; and among the Romans no important action of State was undertaken without the advice of the augers and their pre-occupation with raw liver!

Pliny the Elder attributed the invention of augury to Tiresias the seer of Thebes, and this type of omen-reading was already one millennium old in the time of Classical Greece; the fourteenth-century BCE diplomatic correspondence preserved in Egypt called the 'Amarna correspondence' reveals that the practice was familiar to the king of Alasia in Cyprus who needed an 'eagle diviner' to be sent from Egypt. This earlier, indigenous practice of divining by bird signs, familiar in the figure of Calchas, the bird-diviner to Agamemnon (Homer, *Iliad*, I.69), was largely replaced by divination through inspection of the sacrificial victim's entrails – *haruspices* – during early days of archaic Greek culture. Plato notes that **hepatoscopy** ('liver-gazing') held greater prestige than augury by means of birds.

Both oracles and seers in ancient Greece practiced divination. Oracles were the conduits for the gods on earth; their prophecies were understood to be the will of the gods verbatim and usually communicated to rulers and prominent persons. Seers were interpreters of signs provided by the gods via natural signs and were more numerous than the oracles being highly valued by all Greeks, not just those with the wherewithal to travel to Delphi or other such sites, where *pythiai* perched on stools, inhaling noxious fumes. As it does today, the ancient Greeks made use of various techniques of divinatory practice: either direct or indirect, and, either spontaneous, or artificial.

Direct divination is where and when a seeker might experience divination by way of dreaming and dreams or by way of a temporary experience of madness, or *phrensy* (frenzy), all of these conditions being a state from which an *inspired* recognition of truth is attained. A necessary condition is that the seeker has made an effort to produce a mental or physical state which encourages a flash of insight. These historically attested efforts included sleeping in conditions whereby dreams might be more likely to occur, inhaling certain vapours, the chewing of leaves, drinking of blood, etc.

Under these conditions the seeker may gain the power of prophecy, albeit temporary, that was associated with caves and grottoes within Greek divination, and the nymphs and Pan who were associated with caves often bestowed the gift of prophesy. Pan was able to dwell within people, a condition known as **panolepsy** that causes inspirational abilities relating to divination or prophecy. A degree of possession of an individual by a nymph is known as **nympholepsy**, meaning 'caught by nymphs' … a term we would use today as someone 'being fairy led'.

Indirect divination whereby a seeker observes natural conditions and phenomenon such as 'sortilege', and chance encounters with the animal kingdom. This consists of the casting of lots, or *sortes*, whether with sticks, stones, bones, beans, coins, or some other item and often interpreted by a third party. Modern playing cards and board games are believed to have been developed from this type of divination, whereby dice or counters are cast in order to predict the future.

But not all divinatory methods were well received. As early as 692. the Quinisext Council, also known as the 'Council in Trullo' in the Eastern Orthodox Church, passed canons to eliminate paganism and the practice of divination, but it continued to be popular well into the Middle Ages despite being frequently banned by the Church. In fact the seven *artes magicae* or *artes prohibitae*, i.e. those methods of divination prohibited by canon law (as expounded by Johannes Hartlieb in 1456), were:

- Nigromancy
- Hydromancy
- Aeromancy
- Pyromancy
- Chiromancy
- Scapulimancy
- Geomancy

It has been suggested that the division between the four 'elemental' disciplines (i.e. geomancy (Earth), hydromancy (Water), aeromancy (Air) and pyromancy (Fire) appears to be a contrivance of the time, but traditional forms such as chiromancy was the divination from a subject's palms as practised by the Romany (at the time recently arrived in Europe), and scapulimancy, the divination from animal bones, in particular shoulder blades as practised in peasant superstition. By contrast, nigromancy came from scholarly 'high magic' derived from High Medieval *grimoires* such as the *Picatrix* or the *Liber Rasielis* and was classed as 'black magic' and demonology, by the vernacular etymology, from *necromancy*.

In the constitution of 1572 and public regulations of 1661 of

Kur-Saxony, capital punishment was used on those predicting the future and laws forbidding divinatory practice continue to this day in some parts of the world. Nevertheless, the belief in 'fortune-telling' continued to be looked upon as a popular pastime for finding a husband or predicting a favourable outcome with regards to health, wealth and happiness. Even the popular Victorian compilations of superstitions were given a Christian spin to weed out anything that wasn't considered 'nice' or smacked too much of paganism, but the Folklore Society's extensive archive enables serious researchers to trace these old divinatory practices back to their roots.

Divination, however, is only a small part of a witch's stock in trade and although a very basic introduction to the subject can be learned from books, proficiency will only come through vigorous practice. This proficiency comes through the discovery of certain secret matters by a great variety of means – correspondences, signs and occult techniques – and before a witch can perform any of these operations with any degree of success, we need to develop the 'art of seeing' and the ability to *divine with rod, fingers and birds'*. Adrien, one of our Coven of the Scales students reported his breakthrough by observing:

Animals have much to teach us. If we observe them, they can give us a lot of information. One simple example is in the London Underground. We see many mice. They often run on the tracks but as soon as a train approaches, they run away, way before we can even hear the train. They warn us of the train's arrival. We can also learn how to read omens with animals. I am not going to pretend at this point that I am able to, but I really understand that *all* this is interconnected like a huge spider web and anything on one side, affects something on the other side of the web. I believe animals are completely in tune with that. Animals in our environment help us stay connected to the web of life. They remind me of the side of me

I am continuously forced to forget in a busy city.

Very early in his studies, this student had grasped the fact that the animal world helps us to connect to this new level of being, particularly through birds, which have long been recognised as an effective means of divination. Now that he understood the principles behind the phenomena, he began to find that he was beginning to 'see' more. How many people, for instance, will even notice the mice on the Underground ... but he'd watched them and interpreted their behaviour. How they would always disappear long before the rumble of the train was discernable to human awareness. Once we get into the habit of watching the animal world, we will always have something around us to warn when that 'train' is coming!

The most remarkable thing about divination, of course, is its continued success. And a large number of people who turn to professional readers are impressed by the amazing details 'coming through' from their past – but this isn't what divination is about. In his interview, *Cold Reading: Confessions of a 'Psychic'*, Colin Hunter explained that 'cold reading' is a set of techniques used by mentalists, psychics, fortune-tellers, mediums and illusionists to imply that the reader knows much more about the person than the reader actually does. There are dozens of books on the subject that reveal how, without prior knowledge, a practised cold-reader can quickly obtain a great deal of information by analyzing the person's body language, age, clothing or fashion, hairstyle, gender, sexual orientation, religion, race or ethnicity, level of education, manner of speech, place of origin, etc. Cold readings commonly employ high-probability guesses, quickly picking up on signals as to whether their guesses are in the right direction or not, then emphasizing and reinforcing chance connections and quickly moving on from missed guesses. Even the police and military use the technique during interrogation sessions.

The witch, however, is not so much concerned with the past as with the present and more particularly the future. Of course, our past actions affect the way we view the future but if we ignore the warnings that divination brings concerning the present, we will be doomed to repeat the same mistakes over and over again. We must also remember that regardless of whatever method is used to predict the future; those results are not cast in stone! Divination reveals the future as relating to the past and the present, and what will happen if the warnings are not heeded in order to change things *before* they go wrong. The answer is also subjective to where an individual is standing at the precise moment in time when they pose the question. We're back to the saying: *'You can't change anything but yourself, but in changing yourself, everything changes around you.'* So if you don't like what the results of the reading is telling you … do something about it before it's too late!

As witches we are responsible for our own destiny and a proficiency in our own chosen system of divining gives us a powerful advantage. Experienced practitioners usually prefer to use a single form of divination, and while some methods may prove to be more efficient than others, and some diviners may be more accurate than their fellows, it is traditionally part of a witch's natural ability to be able to divine by *'rod, fingers and birds'*, as the saying goes. After years of practice with any particular system, we find that we can interpret the signs without even having to think about it – it's like receiving a message from an old friend.

The results we get from our endeavours are signs of opportunities to be taken, dangers to be avoided or impending news of change. Here the witch also interacts with Nature to keep close watch on any unusual activities or occurrences that might have any effect on themselves, or those close to them. This is another reason why it is essential for even the most urban of witches to be well versed in natural lore as well as magical lore. It pays to understand the local wildlife, otherwise we might not see that unusual 'something' in an animal's or bird's normal behaviour patterns.

Our native flora and fauna are linked to our magical subconscious and, if we have required any form of divinatory methods to guide us through the subsequent stages of our love life or career, we must be receptive to those responses. For those with a working understanding in the language of magical correspondences, it is easy to grasp how natural the reading of the symbols becomes, and how easy and obvious (in most instances) is the interpretation. For the beginner, however, accept that the answers are not going to appear suddenly in chapter and verse in a book on fortune telling. Divination is more subtle and, more often than not for the inexperienced, irritatingly obtuse!

Reading for others is a common moral and ethical dilemma that is often raised on internet sites and personally I always refuse point blank to indulge in the practice. That has not always been the case. There used to be an unwritten ethic whereby a reader seeing something really nasty in the future was duty bound *not* to reveal what they had seen lurking in the woodshed. And in the words of that old Leonard Cohen song … '*I've seen the future, brother, it is murder!*' I decided it was unreasonable for me to carry the burden of knowledge for strangers and waiting for the other boot to drop, and that has remained my personal code to the present day … *so don't ask.*

If you do wish to read for others then remember not to use your own 'tools' for outsiders' readings as these will become contaminated through use. Keep your own private equipment under lock and key and have a completely different set for public readings – even this should be ritually cleansed after use as each reading will leave a psychic residue behind and contaminate the next person's reading.

On the legal front, the whole ball game changed in 2008 when the Fraudulent Mediums Act (which replaced the 1735

Witchcraft Act) was replaced by the new Consumer Protection Regulations. Caroline Davies, writing in *The Guardian* at the time, observed that a whole list of disclaimers must be added to the fortune-teller's spiel if they are to avoid an avalanche of writs from disgruntled customers. The reason behind the introduction of the new law was because very little in the multimillion-pound psychic industry in Britain is for free, and anyone charging or accepting 'gifts' in exchange for a service is bound by the new regulations. A legal specialist wryly observed: 'Now there is no difference in law between a psychic and a double-glazing salesman.'

Let's face it, there are 'professional' fees charged for all manner of types of divination, including Tarot, psychic readings and clairvoyance – just take a look at the number of classified advertisements in any of the MB&S magazines. According to Office of Fair Trading research, which provided the basis for the new changes, psychic mailings are estimated to have cost gullible Britons £40m in 2006-07, while psychic services via telephone, online and satellite TV keep the tills ringing in the psychics' favour.

In the USA the legal status of spiritualists, psychics, fortune-tellers and healers has often been a precarious one, and explains why many pagans adopted the title of Reverend as this kept them within the boundaries of the law. As one web-post explained: 'If one goes to psychic fairs, etc., you will notice that virtually all readers are Reverend "So and So" with another title attached. If you are using Tarot or scrying for a church or religious purpose [i.e. counselling], and not for the purpose of fortune-telling – you are legal.' So there you have it … if you are a professional diviner and charge a fee for your services, you might be falling foul of the Office of Fair Trading … or you might just be an ordained psychic minister!

From a purely personal point of view, my abilities when it comes to divination, have always been limited, I have to confess.

I regularly use **cartomancy** (i.e. Crowley's Thoth Tarot) and the pendulum for personal divinatory purposes – and with a great deal of success I might add – but tend to rely more on the messages from the natural world on a daily basis. I have the most amazing crystal ball collection but generally use them for meditational work by holding the appropriate sphere in the palm of the hand – one colour for each *sephiroth* of the Qabalah – rather than prediction. So ... I'm okay with fingers (**cleidomancy**) and birds (**alectryomancy**) but the rod (**rhabdomancy**), I *really* have to work at to get any kind of results ...

Chapter Two

Divination by Rod (Rhabdomancy)

The 'rod' refers to the tool used by traditional witches and ritual magicians for conjuring and directing energy. In witchcraft this would be a wand or staff cut from any of the indigenous trees, since each one has particular magical properties that the witch would identify with (see *Root & Branch: British Magical Tree Lore* for a complete listing). And those trees that are traditionally associated with divination or prophesy are:

Beech rods or staffs are used in the magic of divination and help to balance mental health. Aspiration, desire, and victory are all key elements of this wood. Used while working with ancestors, old wisdom, and magical research.

Cherry wands or staffs are extremely centred and possess very grounded energy – unwavering, and solid – so cherry wood is used in ritual to stabilise and focus. It is often used for intuitive and insight and to overcome obstacles. This is an excellent choice for divination or medium work, as well as healing and love magic.

Crab apple is a powerful wand or staff of choice for the witch when working with the Faere magic; a good wood for aiding in the propagation of skills; promotes peace and harmony, magic of light and the divine, and encourages visions.

Hornbeam wands or staffs attract luck, healing, wisdom, divination, clairvoyance and longevity.

Poplar wands or staffs are strong with the elements of hope, rebirth, and divinations.

Wych Elm wands or staffs can be used in magical workings to gain inspiration and insight.

Yew wands or staffs are associated in legend with many magical powers and used as a dowsing rod; the yew can direct the bearer to recover missing treasure or property.

Rhabdomancy is a divination technique which involves the use of any rod, wand, staff, stick, or arrow for prediction purposes, the word coming from the ancient Greek *rhabdos*, meaning wand or stick. The practice has been mentioned in a number of Biblical references: St Jerome connected *Hosea,* 4.12, which reads: '*My people ask counsel at their stocks, and their staff declareth unto them'* to ancient Greek rhabdomantic practices, and Thomas Browne, in his *Pseudodoxia Epidemica,* notes that *Ezekiel,* 21.21 describes the divination by arrows of Nebuchadnezzar II as rhabdomancy, although more accurately it should be classed as **belomancy**. Plato also noted, the *barsom,* or sacred bundle of twigs as a ritual implement, played an important part in Zoroastrian religious practices since prehistoric times and was also a type of wand used for divination.

The most common method of rhabdomancy in the past was setting a number of staffs on end and observing where they fell, to divine the direction one should travel, or to find answers to certain questions. Needless to say, the answers are restricted to 'yes' or 'no' with the relevant direction predetermined prior to casting the staffs. Another method is throwing a stick or staff into the air to see in which direction it will point when it falls: the end that makes contact with the ground when walking should mark the positive response, not the hand-held end. This method was used at the start of the Kurosawa film, *Yojimbo,* when the hero is undecided on which road to take ... and with interesting results.

The term has also been used since ancient times for divination by arrows (which have wooden shafts) – otherwise known as

belomancy – that was practised by the Babylonians, Greeks, Arabs and Scythians, from where it passed to the Slavonians, and then the Germans, whom Tacitus observed made use of it. The word come from the Greek *belos*, meaning 'arrow or dart' and *manteia* meaning 'divination'. The arrows were typically marked with certain symbols and had to have feathers for every method. In one method, different possible answers to a given question were written and tied to each arrow. For example, three arrows would be marked with the phrases, *God orders it me, God forbids it me*, and the third would be blank. The arrow that flew the furthest indicated the answer. Another method involves the same thing, but without shooting the arrows. They would simply be shuffled in the quiver, worn preferably on the back, and the first arrow to be drawn indicated the answer. If a blank arrow was drawn, a redraw would take place. A lost traveller might also use belomancy to find his way, by tossing the arrow into the air, and letting its angle show him the way.

Xylomancy is the ancient art and practice of reading the omens from twigs, pieces of wood, or fallen tree branches by their shape, colour, thickness and size, as well as location, formations and patterns. If one falls suddenly onto the path, a surprise or shock will follow. In early times only wood that had fallen naturally was considered appropriate but later on sticks were stripped of half of their bark and tossed to the ground, forming random patterns. Those that fell bare side up were then prophetically interpreted.

Divination of future events could also be interpreted from the arrangements of logs in the fireplace, with prophetic interpretations made from the manner in which they burned, as well as from the way the logs were positioned in the fire. Other forms of divination related to xylomancy are **dendromancy** and **tephramancy**, which is divination from the ashes of the burned wood, particularly a tree trunk. In Lewis Spences's (1920) *An*

Encyclopaedia of Occultism he writes:

Divination by means of wood, practised particularly in Slavonia. It is the art of reading omens from the position of small pieces of dry wood found in one's path. No less certain presages of future events may be drawn from the arrangement of logs in the fire-place, from the manner in which they burn, etc. It is perhaps the survival of this mode of divination which makes the good people say, when a brand is disturbed, that 'they are going to have a visitor'.

A simple divinatory method is to take two sticks of equal length and strip the bark of one (positive) and leave the other natural (negative). Drop them over a bridge across a river or fast-flowing stream so that they go with the current: the first one to reach the other side gives the answer. Pooh sticks, anyone?

Less commonly, the term rhabdomancy has also been assigned to the Chinese **I-Ching**, which traditionally used a bundle of yarrow stalks to determine the future. Archaeological evidence shows that Zhou dynasty divination was grounded in cleromancy, the production of seemingly random numbers to determine divine intent. The *Zhou yi* provided a guide to cleromancy that used the stalks of the yarrow plant, but it is not known how they became numbers, or how specific lines were chosen from the line readings. Like the *Zhou yi* itself, yarrow stalk divination dates to the Western Zhou period, although its modern form is a reconstruction. The most common form of divination with the *I Ching* in use today is a reconstruction of the method described in these histories, from the third-century BCE *Great Commentary*, and later in the *Huainanzi* and the *Lunheng*. From the *Great Commentary's* description, the Neo-Confucian Zhu Xi reconstructed a method of yarrow stalk divination that is still used throughout the Far East.

Strangely the use of yarrow stalks crops up in a completely different context in Harold Roth's *The Witching Herbs: 13-Essential*

Plants and Herbs for Your Magical Garden and in collections of British folk practices many charms also involve yarrow. Now not many people know this – but the plant is known for being polymorphic – taking many forms in a single species. In other words, as a species, it's a shape shifter and its Latin name for the yarrow's genus is *Achillea* – the name of the Greek warrior who was the son of shape-shifting parents. Each of its forms – *Achillea lanulosa* and *Achillea millefolium* – has a different number of chromosomes and a different profile of volatile chemicals (fragrances) depending on the locale where it grows. So, from plant to plant, one yarrow can have not only a different scent but also different medicinal and magical capabilities.

On the surface the two different uses are completely unrelated but the ancient Chinese also knew a thing or two about plants and their properties. Perhaps yarrow could be used to create an altered state of consciousness for divinatory purposes when consulting the I-Ching. Just a thought ...

Other similar Eastern methods using sticks for divination are 'Chi-Chi' sticks – a fortune-telling practice that originated in China in which the questioner requests answers from a sacred oracle lot. The practice of *Kau Cim* (or called Chinese Fortune Sticks by westerners) is often performed in a Taoist or Buddhist temple in front of an altar and is also sometimes known as 'The Oracle of Kuan Yin' in Buddhist traditions. The flat bamboo sticks that resemble wide, flat incense sticks are often painted red at one end and are stored in a long cylindrical bamboo tube. A single number, both in Arabic numerals and in Chinese characters, is inscribed on each stick. Each stick has a different number on it, and no two are alike. There are usually a total of one hundred sticks in the cup, although the commercial 'Chi Chi' sticks variation sold in the USA for fortune telling has only seventy-eight sticks.

In many cases, an offering is made prior to the asking of the question in order to curry good favour from the higher powers;

these offerings typically consist of incense, fresh fruit, cakes, or monetary donations. After the seeker has finished their devotions to the deity of choice, they purify the cylinder by revolving it around the incense burner three times and mixing the sticks by hand. The seeker kneels in prayer, holding the cup between their palms and asking their question to the deity, either aloud or by whispering. This part needs to be done decisively as one should not shift questions or hesitate on the question in the middle of the rite. The shaking of the cylinder, which is usually tipped slightly downward, results in at least one stick leaving the cylinder and being dropped onto the floor. In most cases, if multiple sticks leave the cylinder, those fortunes do not count and must be shaken again. Each stick, with its designated number, represents one answer. When a single stick falls out, the number will correspond to one of the hundred written oracles that provide the answer the seeker has requested.

In Japan, there are strips of paper or wooden sticks known as *omikuji* that can be found at Shinto shrines and Buddhist temples. Literally meaning 'sacred lot', *omikuji* have fortunes written on them – some good, some bad – and are usually received by making a small offering and randomly choosing one from a box, hoping for a good result. Traditionally, *omikuji* are written in poem form and many are based on the *100 Chinese Poems* written by the Buddhist monk Tendai. A long time ago, the *omikuji* were used as a guidance for decision making, as people wanted to know if their life plans were to be successful or not.

So there we have it. Rhabdomancy appears to be universally applied to any form of fortune-telling or divination that is influenced by the use of wood – either in the form of thin sticks to more substantial wands or staffs. Like most divinatory systems, it is an ancient arte that has been practised since time immemorial and no doubt every type of wood divination has its origins in the primitive, animistic practice of tree worship – one of the earliest forms of religion. Wood, of course, is the natural material of the witch and it symbolises the power of Nature in all her guises and there are probably very few Old Crafters who do not possess a 'rod' albeit in the form of a wand, staff or Coven stang.

Needless to say, all witches have, or should have, an affinity with wood since we're all tree-huggers at heart. The woods were the original pagan temples and who is there amongst us who does not feel a physical pain whenever trees are felled in our location? Our wand or staff is our magical and spiritual connection to those woods and forests even though we may be forced by circumstance to live in an urban environment.

Obtaining a wand or staff

There are specific rules about obtaining wood for a wand or staff and these must be strictly adhered to (see *Traditional Witchcraft for the Woods and Forests*), since digression could result in the magical properties of the rod being negated, or at worst, blighted. And don't be tempted to use fallen or decayed wood because if the tree rejected that particular piece, then there must be a very good reason for it: branches torn from the tree during winter gales or from a tree felled by the storm, however, will retain that taint of violent energy that will be imprinted in the wood. According to Richard Cavendish (*The Magical Arts*), for example: the wand of the ritual magician must be made of hazel and cut at sunrise so that it captures the vigorous energy of the newly reborn sun (i.e. at Winter Solstice).

For the witch's purpose, find and prepare your own magical staff (or wand) from one of those trees listed above, or from an indigenous tree that has an affinity with your own magical persona. Ideally, a wand should be the length measured from the wrist to the elbow; the staff should be of the same height as the person for whom it is intended. Approach the tree at dawn, quietly and in a spirit of deference, and ask permission from the tree before cutting: if the leaves and twigs rustle gently in response you may proceed, if the leaves and twigs become agitated then leave well alone and move on to another tree. Cut the branch as quickly as possible, using secateurs, lopping shears, or a small saw … do not rip a branch from the tree and remember to leave a suitable offering in its place. Take the branch home and trim off any twigs before putting it away somewhere safe and flat to dry.

Those trees mentioned earlier in the text have traditional associations with divination or prophesy – particularly the beech – and your own personal staff (or wand) might be something quite different from the Coven stang. For example, our Coven's totem tree is the Alder but my personal wands have been taken from the Yew and the Blackthorn; and I use their leaves, seeds, fruit and bark for my magical and path-workings, together with the appropriate correspondences for spell-casting and divination. There are, of course, other variations:

- The traditional hazel thumb-stick is also carried by many witches instead of a staff and the preparation differs slightly, in that V-shape at the top should be at eye-level so that it can be used for 'sighting' and divinatory purposes. The thumb-stick can also act as a personal stang for a solitary witch.

- A formal coven stang, however, should be cut from an ash tree and is part of the formal coven regalia; while an unadorned blackthorn stang is used for cursing and banishing. The 'forked' stang is placed at the outside portal of the Circle to act as the guardian and decorated according to the rite being performed, having been consecrated in the name of the four elements.

- Alternatively, an old pitchfork can be used as the Coven stang since the curved metal prongs represent Horned God energy. If you can find one in an old antiques' warehouse

then this must be magically cleansed before being consecrated in order to rid it of any negative energies it may
be harbouring after its years in the magical wilderness. A
rural labourer would have roused no comment if seen out
and about carrying one of the tools of his trade and, as
with all magical equipment of Old Craft, general everyday
working items would be utilised as and when necessary.

- Every stang must be 'shod with iron' and I've found that
old horseshoe nails are perfect for the job. In *Witchcraft: A
Tradition Renewed*, Evan John Jones explained that like a
battery, the stang is charged with magical energy and by
shodding it with iron, the energy is unable to run to earth,
and remains within the 'body' of the stang.

Both my wands came from Wales, cut from the trees that were
part of my everyday life. The yew was stripped down to the raw
wood and its only decoration is a flint arrowhead embedded in
the top. I didn't have much success with it until I accidentally
spiked myself with the tip of the arrow and drew blood; once the
wand had been 'blooded' it became a very powerful weapon in
my witch's arsenal. The blackthorn wand is equally as powerful
but for different reasons since it is a law unto itself; the yew
wand is far more amenable even though they both have those
eerie Otherworld energies and a taste for blood.

Once I had acquired these two (some three years apart), I felt
it was appropriate to dispose of my original ash wand in the
time-honoured fashion.

Disposal

Like the witch's knife, the wand is also a very personal magical
item and should be treated as such, especially if it is one no lon-
ger in use. Should it be necessary for any reason to dispose of a
wooden wand, staff or stang then an ideal solution is to return
to the mother tree (or one of the same species) from which the

tool was cut and bury it deep down among the root system. Staff and stangs can be cut to neutralise their power and then either burned and the ashes scattered around the roots of a tree of the same species; or the short lengths pushed deep into the ground by the roots.

Important: It is not a good idea to use a wand, or any piece of magical equipment belonging to another witch unless it has been bequeathed to you by its owner. This should be borne in mind when disposing of the regalia of a deceased member of the Coven.

How to use the magic wand

Most magical texts agree that the wand should be held in the right hand while praying, or while calling or addressing spirits; and in the left hand when throwing a curse. Professor of Humanities, Christopher A. Faraone gives an ancient Greek spell wherein the divinity or spirit is invoked while holding a branch of laurel in the right hand, and an ebony staff in the left. When dismissing the spirits, the hands are switched. In this instance it was primarily a defensive weapon and used to strike a bowl in some divinatory methods. In Zoroastrian ritual the gaze and the ritual power (*amal*) is focussed on the *barsom* – also held in the right hand.

There is no need to cleanse a staff or wand that has been taken straight from the tree but it is a necessary requirement to consecrate it for magical use. Cast your protective Circle and holding the rod in the right hand, sprinkle it with spring water using a bunch of mint, marjoram, and rosemary tied with thread. Begin by holding the staff or wand up towards the North – the Place of Power – and say:

Oh Great God of the Forces of Nature,
let Thine influence descend and consecrate this staff/wand

which I dedicate to Thee for the performance
Of the works of prophesy and divining thy Will.

You must then kiss the item and, as you do so, know that you are giving the Breath of Life to this magical object. If you can, visualise your kiss breathing a crucial portion of witch-power into the tool – then repeat the evocation at each of the Four Corners. This consecration ritual can be used for any and all of your magical tools as it is necessary to cleanse and consecrate every item to each of the four elements because each tool is a compound of earth, air, fire and water. When not in use, the rod should be kept wrapped in a piece of silk of any colour – except black or brown.

The wand is the symbol of magical Will and is often considered to be the principle weapon of the magical practitioner – a parody of which is the implement used by the stage magician or illusionist. Nevertheless, a wand or rod is one of the supreme emblems of magical power and as was recorded in myth, Circe changes the comrades of Odysseus into swine with her *rhabdos*, or wand.

Divining With Hazel Rods

The most common use of rhabdomancy, of course, is 'dowsing' in its traditional form of using a wooden stick, usually forked – and hazel is well known for its dowsing abilities, even by people with no magical powers whatsoever. Dowsing is a recognised type of divination employed in attempts to locate ground water, buried metals or ores, gemstones, oil, old gravesites, lost property and many other objects and materials without the use of scientific apparatus.

Traditionally, the most common dowsing rod is a forked (Y-shaped) branch from a tree or bush. Some dowsers prefer branches from particular trees, and some prefer the branches to be freshly cut. The forked dowsing rod was traditionally made of a hazel branch because the wood has long been known for its reputed magical properties. Other woods which are reputed to have magical properties include ash, rowan, and willow: also considered excellent for wands. Hazel twigs in Europe and witch-hazel in the United States are commonly chosen, as are branches from willow or even in some instances, peach trees. The two ends on the forked side are held one in each hand with the third (the stem of the Y) pointing straight ahead. The dowser then walks slowly over the places where he suspects the target (for example, minerals or water) may be, and the dowsing rod dips, inclines or twitches when a discovery is made. This method is sometimes known as 'willow witching' or 'water divining'.

For many years speculation was that such movement of the rod was caused by an underground emanation or an 'occult' force. However, as a result of an increased interest in dowsing during the twentieth century, some modern theorists believe the movement of the rod may be caused by a response caused by the dowser's sensitivity to the object for which they are seeking; a theory that does not preclude the possibility of some sort of electro-magnetic impulse which stimulates the muscles in the individual's nervous system.

The Blasting Rod

Even though not directly related to the magical arte of divination, when talking about 'rods' it would be remiss of the author not to mention the subject of 'blasting rods'.

The traditional blasting rod in witchcraft is taken from the blackthorn, a shrub that has a very mixed reputation in British folklore; the blackthorn is most strongly identified with traditional British Old Craft through its long associations with magic and the Faere Folk. It is mentioned in Celtic Brehon Law and is even supposed to have its own special tribe of Faere guardians who will take revenge on anyone cutting a branch from the tree at either the old opening or closing of the year – i.e.

according to the old Julian calendar. Archaeological research has also established that the fruit from the blackthorn – sloes – which are common in the wild were consumed in large quantities as far back as Neolithic times. These ancient references probably explain the deep-rooted fear of the shrub as something that is best avoided since it represents the displaced, indigenous people of these islands. In later times, these ancient people, the Faere Folk and witches, were all said to be ancestors of one and the same.

It is therefore understandable why blackthorn is regarded as a wood of great power and a keeper of secrets due to its near-impenetrable thorns that will turn a wound septic if you get scratched gathering the wood or fruit. It is also considered to have a negative side which was historically used for 'binding and blasting', while witches used them to blight crops and make the livestock of their enemies barren. Blackthorn is also depicted in many fairy tales throughout Europe as a tree of ill omen; it is called *straif* in the Ogham, and has the most sinister reputation in Celtic tree lore. The English word 'strife' is said to derive from this Celtic word. For witches it represents the 'dark' side of the Craft since it is sacred to the Dark, or Crone aspect of the Triple Goddess, and represents the Waning and Dark Moons. Blackthorn is known as 'the increaser and keeper of dark secrets'. The shrub is also linked with warfare, wounding and death, and associated with the Scottish Cailleach – the Crone of Death – and the Irish Morrigan. In Scotland, winter begins when the Cailleach (also Goddess of Winter) strikes the ground with her blackthorn staff – while a sudden cold spell in early spring that prolongs the misery of winter is referred to as a 'blackthorn winter'. A traditional coven will use a blackthorn stang in rituals of cursing and banishing; while the sharp thorns, used to pierce poppets used in curses, were called the 'pins of slumber'. In South Devon folklore, witches were said to carry blackthorn walking sticks, with which they caused much local mischief, although this belief may stem from the Irish shillelagh, a blackthorn stick or cudgel. Typically made from a stout knotty stick with a large knob at the top and associated with Irish folklore, the shillelagh was originally used for settling disputes in a gentlemanly manner – like a duel with pistols or swords – with wood from the root being prized as it was less prone to cracking during use. I have one made for me by an Old Crafter that sits in the umbrella stand by the door in case of intruders! Needless to say, according to Christian folklore, blackthorn is seen as a sinister tree and associated with witchcraft. Witches and heretics were said to have been burned on blackthorn pyres while the Devil was believed to prick his follower's fingers with the thorn of a blackthorn.

When used for a blasting rod, the piece of branch is usually about one foot long, has to be decorated with certain sigils, blessed and charged in a very certain way before it can be used. The rod has to be made of blackthorn because that wood is very, very good at directing negative energy, and *only* negative energy. In contemporary Wicca, however, in accordance with the 'an it harm none' culture, a blackthorn rod is alleged to be 'well suited to reversing harmful spells, casting strong protection spells or deflecting ill will' but basically it's a wand to deliver mini-hexes and cause harm to people.

From a ritual magic point of view, the most powerful blasting rod was the crystal one used by Allan Bennett who worked in a rented back room, unfurnished except for a small table with two or three books and his famous 'blasting rod'. Posterity records that he preferred this to the wands recommended in the Golden Dawn and charged it with a considerable level of magnetism. He would mount it in a wooden handle painted with words of power that could be changed according to the nature of the operation proposed.

According to Aleister Crowley's account, Allan Bennett constructed a magical wand, made from a lustre – a long glass prism with a neck and a pointed knob such as adorned old-fashioned chandeliers, which he carried around with him. Crowley also related the story that he and Bennett were out walking one day and came across a group of theosophists who were ridiculing the use of wands. 'Allan promptly produced his and blasted one of them. It took fourteen hours to restore the incredulous individual to the use of his mind and his muscles.'

As we can see from the various multicultural examples of using 'rods' for divination (and other things besides) that wood is one of the sacred elements of divination that gives birth (fuel) to fire; while fire links the earth with the abode of the gods, who are the ones who will decide on the future Fate of the seeker by either granting or denying the request to see into the future. This is why it is advisable to burn joss sticks or strong wood-based incense when undertaking any form of divination as an aid to concentration, since the hot air carries the perfume upwards towards deity who in turn will – hopefully – grant the gift of 'seeing'.

All incense making begins with the creation of a loose, non-combustible mixture that is simply the combination of two or more ground, granular, powdered, and/or chipped natural aromatic ingredients (herbs, flowers, seeds, spices, woods, bark, gums, resins, etc.). All the ingredients are ground to the consistency of sea salt or coarse sand and an excellent step-by-step guide to creating your own incense can be found at http://incensemaking.com/ with plenty of common sense and practical advice. Such as:

Resins must be ground or powdered in a mortar and pestle. They will clog, destroy and ruin any grinder, mill, blender, processor, etc., you put in their path. The old-fashioned way is still the only way. There are expensive commercial-grade grinders that could do the job but this website is about making incense for personal use. Scoop the entire mixture into a glass jar, seal it closed, label it and let it stand at least overnight in a dark, cool space (a drawer or closet usually works well). The ageing process allows the entire mixture to 'synergize', or merge together as one complex aroma. Ageing for several days or weeks will create a more matured, blended, and complex aroma.

Understanding the correspondences of the fragrances and magical properties of incense will also help focus your mind on achieving specific goals, especially during divination. Commercial incense can be bought loose (to be used with charcoal discs), as joss sticks or cones but may not be readily available to include the woods you require.

Exercise:

Preparing a Beech Rod or Wand for Divinatory Use

To obtain a staff of a suitable length and thickness may prove difficult, however, since a staff should be the same height as the seeker and such branches may well be out of reach; lower branches, however, are ideal for a wand that traditionally should be measured from the user's wrist to elbow. It is interesting to note that while the beech is often described as the 'queen of the woods', those who work with beech staffs and wands maintain that the energies from this tree are most definitely male and aligned with **Elemental Earth**. The beech is also said to be the tree of the Summer Solstice so the perfect time to cut a rod would be at dawn on that day and wash it in the morning dew.

In *The White Goddess*, Robert Graves' footnotes suggest that the Franks and Achaeans originally consulted beech oracles but finding no beeches on their migrations, transferred their allegiances to the oak, the nearest equivalent, to which they gave the name *phegos* – the same word as *fagus*, the Latin for beech. Venantius Fortunatus, a sixth-century bishop-poet wrote: *Barbara fraxineis pingatur runa tabellis* – 'Let the barbarian rune be marked on beech-wood tablets.' Although the beech does not appear among traditional Ogham staves, there is some evidence to suggest that the Germanic/Norse runic alphabet was carved onto beech; the first source being Tacitus's *Germania*, in which he describes 'signs' chosen in groups of three and cut from 'a nut-bearing tree'.

Once the staff/wand has been cut to the right length, and under the correct circumstances (see above), and a suitable offering of cider or port given in thanks, take the wood home and leave it flat on the ground to dry. You can decide whether you wish to leave the wood plain, since beech has a beautifully smooth grey bark – or strip it and decorate it with magical runes. Providing no one else has handled the staff (or wand), magical cleansing will not be necessary as it will still carry the essence of the parent tree. Once you decide it is ready for use, consecrate the rod using the rite suggested above. The beech wand or staff should be used in all rites of divination or learning, and for welcoming in the Summer Solstice.

Chapter Three

Divination by Fingers (Sortilege)

Divination using the fingers, relies on the sensation of touch combined with the use of the many ancient sortilege systems – which is a 'prognostication employing objects with sides that are cast or drawn'. This form of divination originated more than 5000 years ago, when the first pebbles, twigs, shells or bones were thrown on the ground and the tribal shaman interpreted the meaning from the pattern created when they fell. According to *The Book of Divining the Future*, Eva Shaw explains that all forms of sortilege take place when an object is thrown into the air, dropped on the ground, or selected from a bag or box.

As with ming sticks, rune stones, tarot cards and other divination with playing cards and dice are considered by some to be sortilege systems because of the random selection. Sortilege systems are utilised to determine future happenings or interpret omens, and they cross all geographical and cultural lines.

Needless to say, there are numerous methods of divination that fall into this area and so it is not surprising that our fingers certainly do the walking when it comes to selecting our favourite technique for predicting the future. It also offers the most ancient, popular and easiest forms of the practice, for example:

Astragyromancy is divination of the future or the answer of a seeker's question employing objects with sides. Ancient practitioners used knucklebones and the root word, *astragalos,* is Greek for vertebra or knucklebones.

Cartomancy is divination using a pack of cards (including the

Tarot) to predict the future or to respond to a question.

Cleidomancy is divination using the swinging of a pendulum to foretell the future or answer the seeker's questions.

Cleromancy is divination using objects with sides which are thrown on a table onto a cloth with specific divination markings.

Crystallomancy is an ancient divination practice of casting lots using small stones or small crystals.

I-Ching using coins (instead of yarrow stalks) is a Chinese system of divination said to have originated well before written time prior to 2498 BCE. Composed of 64 three-line patterns made up of broken and unbroken lines, the answers are provided by *The Book of Changes.*

Icosahedron were known from Graeco-Roman times as a form of divination by the rolling of a twenty-sided 'dice' to discover which deity should be appealed to for a favourable outcome.

Ogham is known as the Irish tree alphabet and originally used by the Celts and Picts for inscriptions. It is now a popular method of divination.

Runes are a Germanic system of divination deriving their name from the word *raunen,* meaning a secret or mystery. Marked with a mystical symbol they were in use in Europe long before recorded time. The use spread throughout the German and Scandinavian peoples and were in regular use as a divinatory tool by CE 100.

Psychometry is prognostication through holding an object belonging to someone who is not present.

It should be stated quite categorically at this point, that a witch cannot be expected to excel at all these different methods of divination. We need to discover which one is best suited to our own individual abilities and strive to perfect it, rather than run around like a sorcerer's apprentice in a magical sweetshop. With the exception of **psychometry** (which is a gift), the rest can be learned in a relatively short time but what takes years of practice is the ability to *correctly interpret* the random selection of the cards, dice and stones at the many different psychic levels of consciousness.

Many of these sortilege systems are now commercially produced and come with an instruction manual that may have its uses in reaching an understanding of the basic meanings. But these take no account of the *personal* connection we may have with the numerous magical correspondences and images – particularly individual crystals, stones and specific Tarot cards. Once we begin to find our way around a system when reading for ourselves we often discover that the 'instruction manual' is completely at odds with what a particular crystal, stone or card is *telling* us on an inner level – this is where the arte and craft of magic comes into the equation! We can't always take as gospel the instructions given in a book!

The Power of the Pendulum

For example, my fingers are best suited to **cleidomancy** and over the years I have experimented with numerous different types and sizes of pendulum made of different materials. Magically, a pendulum is a weight suspended from a pivotal cord or chain so that it can swing freely; scientifically when a pendulum is displaced sideways from its resting, equilibrium position, it is subject to a restoring force due to gravity that will accelerate it back toward the equilibrium position. Generally speaking, a pendulum is a small weight on a cord or chain. And that's all it is! It can be any weight, and it can be any sort of cord or chain.

The pendulum itself is, more often than not, an object only about ½ inch by 1 inch in size and the cord or string is about 8 inches long; the whole thing fitting easily in a small pocket or pouch.

Like dowsing with hazel twigs, from earliest times, pendulums have been used to locate water, gold, gems, and other valuable commodities – as well as missing items. In Europe early scientists and doctors would consult a pendulum for medical diagnoses to locate infections and weak areas of the body and to determine the gender of unborn infants. In the practice of radiesthesia, a pendulum is used today for medical diagnosis.

People also trust the pendulum enough to let it guide them through the most difficult times of their lives. For an extreme example, during WWII, a pendulum was used by Colonel Kenneth Merrylees to locate deeply buried bombs. He was employed by the Army to dowse water supplies for Allied troops at the front, and also worked as a bomb disposal expert back home, where he used his dowsing skills to find unexploded bombs with delayed-action fuses that had penetrated deep into the ground; famously locating one 500-pounder under the swimming pool at Buckingham Palace. Even the most hard-bitten sceptic is not going dismiss the Colonel's remarkable abilities with his pendulum!

Another advocate of *The Power of the Pendulum* (published in 1976) was T.C. Lethbridge, an English archaeologist, parapsychologist, and explorer. A specialist in Anglo-Saxon archaeology, he served as honorary Keeper of Anglo-Saxon Antiquities at the Cambridge University Museum of Archaeology and Ethnology and over the course of his lifetime wrote twenty-four books on various subjects, becoming particularly well known for his dowsing and other experiments with a pendulum.

It is usual practice to first determine the response you will be using: (i.e. left-right, up-down); which will indicate 'yes' and which 'no' before proceeding to ask the pendulum specific questions. The pendulum may also be held over a pad or cloth with 'yes' and 'no' written on it, or perhaps other words written in a circle. The person holding the pendulum aims to hold it as steadily as possible over the centre and its movements are believed to indicate answers to the questions. Repeatedly asking the same question should be avoided as pendulums have been known to become ratty and climb up the cord like a snake about to strike!

Quite simply, when held correctly, the pendulum reacts to very small nerve reactions in our fingers that are generated by our unconscious mind in response to a question. Different nerve reactions will be detected depending on what our subconscious mind knows. These reactions are transmitted to our fingers from the deep recesses of the mind and through our fingers to the cord holding the weight of the pendulum. These tiny nerve transmissions affect the cord and are then transmitted to the weight – causing it to move in some direction. So rid yourself of the myth that a pendulum is moved by some spirit, or by magic – it is moved by our subconscious mind ...

Yet! There is a certain amount of magic in the ability to interpret some of the reactions. I have found that the best results come from a pendulum with some quartz content since this is the mineral that 'earths' our magical abilities and makes the link with those chthonic energies that set the pendulum swinging ... backwards and forwards for 'yes' ... in a circle for 'no' ... although others may use the opposite interpretation. We make sure we're on the same wavelength by uttering a simple incantation like: *'Adonai, please answer my questions. Swing backwards and forwards for 'yes' or in a circle for 'no'. I thank you'.*

My personal pendulum is a heavy crystal droplet from an old chandelier. Despite its name, 'crystal' is actually glass containing a minimum of twenty-four per cent lead. Not present in other types of glassware, the lead increases the sparkle and makes it easier to cut; the brilliance of lead crystal relies on the high reflective qualities caused by this lead content. Although these droplets are manufactured there is still enough lead content to link us with the earth and its magical correspondences. I also use a heavy pendulum because it takes more than a slight nervous reaction to set it swinging, and also for it to change from swinging backwards and forwards, to rotating in a circle without any detectable sensation of movement within the hand in response to my questions.

In addition, in alchemy lead is known as the silent metal. It is a law unto itself and in magic creates a space of silence; this is the perfect metal for 'infinite space' meditations, making an effective barrier against all forms of negative energy. Ruled by Saturn, the magical use of lead promotes contact with deep unconscious levels (both the underworld and Otherworld), deep meditation, banishing negativity breaking bad habits and addictions, protection, stability, grounding, solidity, perseverance, concentration and conservation.

The magical correspondences also include: the astrological houses of Capricorn and Aquarius; Chronos, the father of Time; the Universe in the Major Arcana; the colours black and blue-black; magical powers of malediction and death (since lead is highly toxic), alchemy and geomancy; perfumes – all dull and heavy odours including sulphur and asafoetida.

It is not surprising therefore that a 'crystal' pendulum with its high lead content makes the perfect tool for divinatory work. For the record, my second choice would be a clear quartz crystal with bands of rutile, since quartz (in all its forms) is the most magical mineral on the planet. Although in magical circles we are warned to 'never haggle over a black egg', a large droplet from a broken down chandelier can be obtained for a few pounds off e-Bay, while a decent sized quartz/rutile pendant could have set me back over £100.

Let's face it, divination is both a skill and an arte but an individual's proficiency depends on regular practice just as much as his or her natural abilities. Most witches do, of course, have a particular favourite divining tool, which acts as a prompt for tuning in to psychic forces and if you already have a favourite method, then there is absolutely no reason to change. Just as the good all-rounder is rare in any walk of life, so the witch who can divine by using every tool imaginable is a rare animal indeed! In addition, there are also different types of 'tool'. For example, there now are hundreds of different Tarot packs to choose from and it won't be until you find the design that 'talks' to *you* that you will excel in spontaneous Tarot readings for yourself.

As with all elements of Craft the more we understand about the history and antecedents of our chosen divinatory method, the easier it becomes to instantly get onto our 'contacts' regardless of the technique we are using. It isn't enough to buy a modern book off Amazon and slavishly follow the directions. We need to understand the history behind the system and to discover where it has travelled from to re-emerge in twenty-first- century western esoteric writing. We need to re-connect with the ancient seers, shaman and augers of the ancient world.

For example, one of the most fascinating divinatory tools is the icosahedron.

The Die Is Cast

A rare limestone Egyptian icosahedron dating from the first century CE was not inscribed with Latin or Greek letters or numbers, but with twenty Egyptian divine names that were presumably used in an oracular procedure intended to establish which deity would provide help to the petitioner. (EES, *Journa,l* 2007, Vol.93) An icosahedron is formed by twenty equilateral triangles with twenty divine names written on the sides – on each face, a divine name was written in black ink with the sides outlined in the same. The gods' names were as follows:

1. *Imn* – Amun
2. *P3-Re* – Pre

3. *Pth* – Ptah
4. *Dhwtj* – Thoth
5. *Itm* – Atum
6. *Hprj* – Khepri
7. *Gb* – Geb
8. *Wsjr* – Osiris
9. *Hr* – Horus
10. *3s.t* – Isis
11. *B3s.t* – Bastet
12. *H'pj* – Hapy
13. *T3-Rpy* – Triphis*
14. *Sy* – Shai
15. *Nb.t-H.t* – Nephthys
16. *Nj.t* – Neith
17. *Spsy.t* – Shepshit
18. *Mn* – Min
19. *Hnsw* – Khonsu
20. *Mw.t* – Mut

NB: *Triphis is depicted as a lioness-headed woman wearing a crown with disk, horns and plumes like that of Hathor . Her consort is Min and Triphis is sometimes depicted standing behind Min, touching with her hand the flail which appears over his upraised hand, indicating their intimacy as well as her participation in Min's power.

An icosahedron could be carved from a variety of materials and the Egyptian pantheon provides no obvious pattern for distributing the twenty names; what mattered was the result obtained when the die was thrown and which god was identified in the process.

   Numbered icosahedra were used in Alexandria in games of chance but evidently someone whose pantheon was Egyptian adopted this foreign form, presumably to function as an oracular device. The deity identified by throwing a die could be a possible solution to the problem. It was suggested that the 'Egyptian' icosahedron could perhaps be linked with the 'oracular spells' in the Greek and Demotic magical papyri, although they are later in date; in these an array of different gods are called upon to assist the practitioner and the icosahedron could have been used to decide which deity, or which spell might be used.

Over 2,300 years ago Plato assigned the icosahedron to represent the element of water, and it is said to offer help in balancing the emotions. The shape was said to embody the Sacred Geometry that is believed to be the secret language of the Universe: Sacred Geometry is found in nature, in art, and in ancient civilizations. It is found in the grand design of the cosmos and is thought, by many, to be the language of the Creator, therefore connecting with Sacred Geometry (via the icosahedron) is said to wake up the sleeping memory of our true, infinite selves.

It is possible to purchase low cost wooden or plastic icosahedra from e-Bay (or more expensive quartz crystal ones), which are perfect for creating your own authentic divination tool. With black paint or a fine-tipped felt pen the triangles can be outlined and a deity's name written on each face. Once you begin to understand the many-faceted personalities of the individual gods, a throw of the die will reveal which of them should be petitioned for their help. Substitute the names of those deities less familiar to you with more popular characters from your own pantheon if you wish. Since this is a magical tool, do not be tempted to use it on behalf of others and when it is not in use, keep it hidden away and wrapped in a silk square.

The important thing to remember, however, is that as with all kinds of divination the future is not fixed. Whenever we randomly cast our lots the future is being revealed in the form of a warning that a given set of circumstance *may* happen *if* we don't take steps to prevent it by taking decisive action. A friend of mine regularly used a three-card Tarot draw and then gave up because she kept getting the Tower and the Death cards. She was convinced that something awful was about to happen when in fact both these cards were heralding drastic change, and dependent on the meanings of the other two. And nothing would convince her otherwise. As it turned out the cards were merely warning her that an unexpected change of location (for the better, as it happens) was in the offing!

If we only choose to take a superficial approach towards divination and, let's say for example, we buy a copy of George Hulskramer's *I-Ching in Plain English*, do we *really* expect to get immediate results when we throw our coins onto the table without any understanding of the ancient culture that spawned the technique? *I-Ching* (*The Book of Changes*) is one of the most ancient writings in world literature and, according to Hulskramer, although it was first recorded around the eleventh century BCE, according to tradition the origin of this book of Chinese wisdom goes even further back in time.

Similarly, Adrien (who is, incidentally, French born) with his spider's web also had a sudden insight concerning his choice of Tarot. He said:

I bought my first deck with pocket money when I was a kid. It was the Marseille deck and through the years I have come back to it and gone away again. These past months, as I dug deeper within, an important realisation came to me. I have been trying to experiment for years with non-Marseilles-based decks in order to expand my views and learn about correspondences within the different decks. I finally came to the conclusion that I don't need to look elsewhere. The Tarot has always been with me and it's the Marseille deck; this realisation has pushed me to re-evaluate my thoughts and beliefs about the Tarot de Marseille and why I have decided to go back to this French system.

Again this was a very insightful response because each Tarot deck has a different appeal and it is the design, content and symbology that speak to us on a very personal level in order to influence our choice. There are no standard pictures or presentation, and even the attributes, may vary from deck to deck. The understanding of the Tarot is to liken it to getting to the core of an onion, and as we begin to grasp it on one level, we strip away a layer and ascend to the next level. The study of any one particular system can take years but it provides endless fascination and is extremely rewarding – but not if we keep swapping from one design to another.

Cartomancy: The Tarot

Long before I joined Coven of the Scales I had discovered the fabulous Thoth Tarot (with Aleister Crowley's accompanying *The Book of Thoth)* which, it transpired was the key to delving deeper into his magical teachings. The deck was painted by artist Lady Frieda Harris who had little or no previous knowledge of the Tarot but:

> *She forced him to undertake what is to all intents an original work, including the latest discoveries in modern science, mathematics, philosophy, and anthropology; in a word to reproduce the whole of his Magical Mind pictorially on the skeleton of the ancient Qabalistic tradition ... the anticipated three months' work extended to five years ... She had to work from his very rough sketches, often from mere descriptions, or from reading between the lines of the old packs.*

The door swung open with the merest touch of a finger. A full Tarot pack consists of 78 cards: 56 cards of the Minor Arcana divided into four suits of wands, clubs, pentacles and cups (including the court cards) and 22 trumps of the Major Arcana, which consists of universal archetypal symbols. Familiarise ourselves with the archetypes represented and we won't go far wrong in beginning to learn the esoteric meaning of the cards – and a lot more else besides.

One or possibly two of these Major Arcana cards will quickly identify itself as your own personal card(s) and will always have a significant meaning for you personally, regardless of the others in the spread, or where in the draw it is placed. This will also be a card on which you can focus for meditation since all of the Major Arcana represents portals on the different Paths on the Tree of Life.

The following is a simple Tarot spread called the Celtic Cross using only cards from the Major Arcana. Shuffle the cards and make into a fan in the left hand, and with the right hand pick the eight cards (except number six) at random and place them face upwards in the following order:

This layout should be centralised and the numbers in line with the original or it doesn't make sense.

4

6 2 1 3, 7

5

8

1. Relating to the subject itself.
2. Place to the left (spiritual/emotional) aspect
3. Place to the right (temporal/mundane) aspect
4. Place above the subject
5. Place below the subject
6. Card of spiritual/emotional influences – Add the numbers of all the cards together and reduce the total to its lowest denomination, i.e. if the sum total is 69 added together = 15; added together = 6. Place to the left. If card number 6 has already been drawn it should be taken as doubly en-

forcing the value of that card for spiritual/emotional matters. Leave the space empty or use one of the 'blank' cards.

7. Card of temporal/mundane influences – Re-make the fan
in the left hand and draw the third temporal/mundane
card and place to the right.

8. The 'heel' card.

Reading:

- You should have already discovered your own 'special
card' and this gives a positive outcome to the reading – the
rest merely enforce the strength or impact of the overall
outcome.

- Card number 8 is the 'heel card' that kick-starts the whole
reading, having a direct influence on card number 5 (the
catalyst) and then card number 1. Card number 4 is an
indication of the final outcome.

- Cards 6 and 2 affect the spiritual/emotional aspects of the
subject (i.e. Card 1).

- Cards 3, 7 affect the temporal/mundane aspects of the subject (Card 1).

- The final outcome of the reading (Card 4) obviously depends on the meaning of each individual card and the
type of deck being used.

Meaning:

The central pillar reveals what is likely to happen if all the
energies are flowing in the correct/positive direction. The cards
to left indicate how your actions will affect you spiritually/
emotionally; while the cards to the right reveal how your actions
will affect you on a temporal or mundane level. For every action
there is a reaction on both levels. Remember that the future is
not fixed and that the 'outcome' can be a warning that things
may not go well if the warnings are not heeded.

The Tarot, of course, has no authentic part to play in traditional witchcraft but since we all appear to have a fascination for the system, again, it would be remiss of me to exclude it since the cards are chosen at random by the fingers. Divination by 'fingers' points us in the direction of taking control of our own destiny and not leaving anything to chance – and it is remarkably successful in all its different forms.

Exercise

The Casting of Lots

For this exercise we are going to combine two of the divinatory techniques mentioned above:

cleromancy using objects with sides that are thrown on a table onto a cloth with specific divination markings, and **crystallomancy** using small stones or crystals. (Taken from *Magic Crystals, Sacred Stones* and *CRONE!*)

To begin ... when sitting on a garden seat or park bench look at the stones around your feet. At first glance this will probably appear as ordinary gravel or aggregate from a builders' merchant or garden centre – smooth pebbles or rough-quarried stone. Having said that, pebbles and stones are to be found everywhere: in the shallow stream bed, on the sandy banks of an inland river, turned over in a ploughed field, on the beach, or even dug up in our own gardens. And it isn't necessary to acquire a degree in geology to collect 'magical' pebbles because our choice is reliant on a small stone that catches our eye because of its unusual colour or shape regardless of what it is.

- Each stone may be discovered under unusual circumstances, or it may be something that we just feel the need to pick up and possess. Whatever the reason for our selection, these stones will begin to form the basis for our magical collection. Take your time and add one from a different location whenever you see or feel something special.

- Because these small stones are 'special', you will remember exactly where and under what circumstances you found them. **This is important**. Keep them together in a tall glass vase or small goldfish bowl until you have sufficient quantity to utilise for magical use. Keep a note of each one in a magical journal or diary if you have a poor memory.
- For magic use, always collect small pebbles between the size of your thumbnail and the top joint of your thumb. To begin with, we all make the same mistake of trying to find near-perfect round pebbles but what we should be looking for are ovoids and discs, as well as the weird and wonderful.

Once your magical collection has filled your container to the halfway mark, you are ready to create your own personal system of crystallomancy. The next step is to create a linen cloth for divinatory purposes – using three circles to represent the past, present and future.

- Take a large white linen napkin and in the centre draw a circle the size of a large dinner plate; now place a tea plate in the centre of the first circle and draw a second circle; finally take a teacup or mug and draw a third circle inside the second circle. The centre circle represents Past, the inner circle the Present, and the outer circle the Future.
- Now select 12 small pebbles from your collection. Remember that each stone has been discovered under unusual circumstances, or is one that you just felt the need to pick up and possess. Whatever the reason for your selection, these small stones are 'special', so you will recall exactly where and under what circumstances you found

them – what their significance has for *you*, and how they will influence your 'reading'.

- Holding the 12 stones cupped between the palms of your hands, drop them onto the cloth and observe how they scatter. Disregard any that fall outside the outer circle. Those in the centre circle will refer to the past, which may have a bearing on the present and the future. The stones in the middle circle refer to the here and now; those in the outer circle are linked to the future.

- Now begin your first reading by identifying what each stone means to you personally, i.e. good or bad news, travel or a special event. Your subconscious will guide your interpretation. Remember, the 'lots' are deciphered according to the influence of the stones and their placement within the circles – revealing the future as relating to the past and the present, and what will happen if the warnings are not heeded in order to change things *before* they go wrong.

The most remarkable thing about this kind of divination is its overwhelming success – but before setting yourself up as a 'seer' for other people, you will need to create a completely separate set of stones or cards from those used for your own personal readings to avoid unwanted psychic transference. Remember that the future is not fixed, and any advanced warning enables us to make the necessary changes to our lives before anything takes a turn for the worse.

Chapter Four

Divination by Birds (Ornithomancy)

Divining the future by watching birds is one of the most ancient of practices, and even as I'm writing these words, the kestrel flew from the west and passed overhead and continued towards the east where it stopped to hover over the ground. On the following two days, the same bird flew from the north and made a failed attempt to take one of the colony of sparrows from the top of the pine tree, and then appeared to the south while hunting. The kestrel is a regular visitor so his presence wasn't surprising but a sighting on three consecutive days and at the four points of the compass was enough to trigger my responses.

Now raptors, particularly those of the *falconidae* family, have always had a special meaning for me and I judge this to be a warning of sorts. It also means that there will not be any sudden surprises since I will be on my guard against any unexpected happenings. Needless to say there are other factors to be considered but it merely illustrates how warnings come through from Otherworld. Once we have recognised that this is indeed a warning, it often transpires that the potential protagonist picks up on the astral that their intensions have been revealed and they receive a psychic warning: *'Don't even think about it!'*

Another message came with the sighting of a buzzard gliding on the thermals of a warm April afternoon. Living in Wales, where buzzards were relatively common, you could hear their mewling cries and watch them soaring overhead throughout the day. They were part and parcel of everyday life and that call was one of the things I missed most when I moved to England before coming to Ireland. The birds became extinct in Ireland in the late nineteenth century but naturally re-colonised in the early 1930s and have been spreading steadily south and west ever since. However, they are still relatively scarce down in the south of the country. I watched this one circling high above, its distinctive shape silhouetted against the white clouds for about twenty minutes as it circled lazily, the spring breeze gradually taking it further away to the west. I've always had a soft spot for buzzards. I spent years watching them in Wales and they were always magical birds for me. So I take it as a good omen that this one has appeared while all the changes are going on.

I have also mentioned in *CRONE!* about the encounters with members of the *corvidae* family; in themselves none of the sightings necessarily meant anything but I learned a long time ago not to ignore messengers from Otherworld – particularly magpies and crows, since all corvids are highly intelligent, and are among the most intelligent of all animals. Persistent, repeated or unusual behaviour is noted, mentally filed away until, eventually, the penny drops. Funnily enough, I don't usually find I get anything through as a result of flinging myself in and out of Circle, or via divination on these occasions, but rather if I've been mulling things over in my head for a couple of days the meaning will become clear.

In the case of the magpie's behaviour I happened to mention the visits to an Elder of the Coven who promptly replied that the messages probably referred to a matter we've been discussing relating to the proposed changes to the running of the Coven. I thought about what she'd said and it came to me that since magpies are communal creatures, their presence *was* probably referring to the group, and that their close proximity suggested a positive outcome. As we often say: who teaches the teacher!

As far as the crow was concerned, the question I'd been agitating over was whether to make an offering (sacrifice) to something that was important to me, and that would require making a sizeable contribution if the offer was accepted. The act of sharing with the crow, and the bird's acceptance told me that I should go ahead and do what I felt was right.

In another instance, one of the Coven Elders and I were strolling by the river discussing certain developments that were in the offing and, as if in answer to our questions, a heron that had been perched on the castle ramparts flew off. Instead of flying over the bridge, the heron flew into one of the darkened arches and out the other side to perch on the edge of the weir – and provided an answer to our dilemma. An Old Craft witch needs to be on her contacts at all times or the message could have been overlooked.

I suppose there are those who would claim these encounters stem from an overactive imagination or wishful thinking, but they've never steered me wrong in all the years I've relied upon them. Being a country person I suppose observing and reading avian behaviour is second nature but there are plenty of different birds to be found in the inner towns and cities to act as messengers if we take the time to watch them.

There are various methods of divination by birds that date back to the beginning of recorded time. For example:

Alectryomancy refers to divination involving the behaviour of wild and domestic animals, particularly poultry.

Apantomancy is divination by chance or unexpected encounters with animals.

Augury is the practice from ancient Roman religion of interpreting omens from the observed flight of birds (*aves*); when the individual, known as the augur, interpreted these signs, it was referred to as 'taking the auspices' from the Latin *auspicium* and *auspex*, literally 'one who looks at birds'.

Ornithomancy is the divination by the observance of flying birds or through birds' songs.

Theriomacy is a less common name for divination by studying the behaviour of animals and birds.

Birds, being regarded as messengers of higher powers, or as possessors of secret knowledge and serving as oracles and guides guaranteed that certain birds were always associated with divination from prophetic chickens to the flight of the mighty eagle.

For the Egyptians, the grey heron was associated with the sacred *benu*-bird, the prototype of the Greek phoenix and the symbol of the sun and rebirth – the concept of regeneration in the living image of renewed life in divinatory terms. It is not known whether the owl was considered a lucky or unlucky bird but its image is the only one shown full face in the hieroglyphic system. The owl symbolised 'black' which represented both night/ darkness and the 'black land' of Khem so it could hardly have been considered 'evil'. The ibis was regarded as an incarnation of Thoth (Tahuti) the god of wisdom and it was an offence to kill one of these birds. Needless to say, the discovery of a feather from one of these sacred creatures would have been regarded as a sign of great importance and would have had the recipient scurrying along to the temple for an interpretation.

More than 2,400 years ago, the Etruscan seers used a hen or rooster to predict the future by drawing a circle on the ground around which were drawn the twenty letters of the Etruscan alphabet. A kernel of grain was placed in front of each letter and the hen or cock bird was placed within the circle and allowed to peck up the grain. As the bird ate the grain the seer noted the sequence of the letters next to the kernels to answer the seeker's question.

For the Greeks, an *oionos* (omen) was defined as the carnivorous vulture, a particularly prophetic bird. By careful observation of the bird's cries and the way or direction it flew, the augurs attempted to predict the future; when they saw vultures from the left they considered it a bad omen. The cry of a heron to the right marked a positive and promising omen. The Romans employed augers to interpret the appearance of their flight and species but unlike the Greeks, considered that signs from the left were usually favourable and positive, while signs from the right were seen as adverse and negative.

In ancient Rome, augers divined the future using birds: the route the birds flew, their speed, their species and number, along with the sounds made in flight or when they landed. Eva Shaw recorded an intriguing snippet that the augers never actually watched the birds but sat on a nearby hill – often blindfolded – and had their assistants explain what was happening to them. Depending upon the birds, the auspices from the gods could be favourable or unfavourable (*auspicious* or *inauspicious*). Sometimes bribed or politically motivated augurs would fabricate unfavourable auspices in order to delay certain state functions, such as elections.

Birds flying to the east, towards the sunrise, were considered propitious while those flying towards the west and the sunset (in the direction of the underworld) were inauspicious. If they flew low and hither and thither it was unpropitious for it indicated that they were agitated or troubled. It was necessary to distinguish between much activity (or *energeia*), and a steady horizontal formation (or *hedra*), the former telling of strong action while the latter suggested a steady purposefulness. These instructions were applied to the behaviour of separate birds, or to just two or three together, as well as to larger formations.

The songs, cries or calls of birds were also considered to have prophetic meaning and such beliefs survived late into the middle of the twentieth century among country people, fishermen and sailors. For example, if swallows do not return yearly to the eaves of a house it foretells ruin will come to it and here in the Glen, people still wait anxiously for the swallows to return and provide a topic of conversation since their cries are the sound of the start of summer. If they dart so low as to nearly touch the ground summer storms will spoil the crops; if they are soaring high it predicts drought.

Seagulls inland mean a tempest at sea, although colonies of them appear to have relocated to the municipal rubbish tips that provide easier pickings; a lone seabird inland means bad news. The cooing of doves in the wood in the evening is a warning against thieves, but in the dovecote of trees around the house, it promises happiness and prosperity. Flights of wild swans or wild ducks mean travel or news, but if the birds are flying towards the moon the meaning is loneliness, or news of a death.

If, however, we study the various collections of European folklore, we usually find that those birds whose appearance is deemed evil or unlucky are the ones that were considered to be 'messengers' in the Old Ways. According to *Fauna Britannica*:

> There are few birds as obvious, noisy and imposing as the six characteristic black species of this [Corvidae] family, nor are the Magpie and Jay likely to be overlooked. They are highly intelligent and are often thought the most advanced and long-lived of all birds. All eight are residents and their biology and, to a large degree, their extensive folk-lore are similar, so it is difficult to relate many of the older beliefs to any particular species.

The poor old **Raven**, for example, gets a lot of bad press but in reality this bird is one of the oldest symbols of the ancient Britons, being associated with the Welsh god Bran the Blessed whose name translates to 'raven'. According to the *Mabinogion*, Bran's head was buried in the White Hill of London as a talisman against invasion and gave rise to the legend that if the ravens were removed from the Tower of London, then England would fall – King Arthur is alleged to have ignored the warnings and removed the head: later Britain suffered the ignominy of the

Norman invasion.

Because of its black plumage, croaking call, and diet of carrion, the raven has long been considered a bird of ill omen and of interest to creators of myths and legends. Ravens, which were notorious for gathering at gallows, were once abundant in London and often seen around meat markets (such as nearby Eastcheap) feasting for scraps, and may have roosted at the Tower from earlier times. For an Old Craft witch the sighting of a raven in the wild would be seen as bringing an important message from Otherworld in answer to our prayer.

If swallows are the voice of summer, then **Rooks** are certainly the voice of winter in the countryside. The call is usually described as *kaah* – similar to that of the carrion crow, but usually much flatter in tone. It is given both in flight and while perched, when the bird characteristically fans its tail and bows on each caw. Calls in flight are usually given singly, in contrast to the carrion crow's which are in groups of three or four. Solitary birds often 'sing' apparently to themselves, uttering strange clicks, wheezes and human-like notes.

We can divine the answer to our questions by addressing the rook and waiting for the number of caws in response – one for 'yes' and two for 'no'. One of the most magical of winter sights are a colony of rooks 'tumbling' through the air against a blue sky as they ride the thermals and then falling towards the ground, yelling and shouting and displaying their *joie de vivre*. The rook is a bird worth getting to know.

Carrion and **Hooded Crows** are considered to be the same species but they differ in appearance depending on the location. The carrion crow is a handsome glossy black bird while the hooded crow has a slate-grey back and under-parts, and is generally found in Scotland and Ireland or as a coastal winter visitor around the coasts. For magical and divinatory purposes, they should be considered the same. The rook is generally gregarious and the crow solitary, but rooks occasionally nest in isolated trees, and crows may feed with rooks; moreover, crows are often sociable in winter roosts. The most distinctive feature is the voice. The rook has a high-pitched *kaah*, but the crow's guttural, slightly vibrant, deeper croaked *kraa* is distinct from any note of the rook.

The carrion crow is noisy, perching on the top of a tree and calling three or four times in quick succession, with a slight pause between each series of croaks. The wing-beats are slower, more deliberate than those of the rook. Carrion crows can become tame near humans, and can often be found near areas of human activity or habitation including cities, moors, woodland, sea cliffs and farmland where they compete with other social birds for food in parks and gardens.

In Celtic folklore, the crow appears on the shoulder of the dying Cú Chulainn, and could also be seen as a manifestation of the Morrígan. This idea has persisted and the hooded crow is associated with the Faere Folk in the Scottish highlands and Ireland; in the eighteenth century, Scottish shepherds would make offerings to them to keep them from attacking sheep. In Faroese folklore, an unmarried girl would go out on Candlemas morning and throw a stone, then a bone, then a clump of turf at a hooded crow – if it flew over the sea, her husband would be a foreigner; if it landed on a farm or house, she would marry a man from there, but if it stayed put, she would remain unmarried. Since crows are very vocal we can engage them in conversation in a similar manner to that described for the rook.

Magpies are gregarious creatures although they are extremely distrustful of humans. Modern folklore rarely has anything positive to say about them such as one foraging alone in the springtime foretells bad weather and one resting on a house, particularly near a window, foretells a death in the household *'One for sorrow* ... etc.'. But like the rest of the corvid family, these are highly intelligent birds despite the hysterical cackling when someone tells a good joke! Because of their distrust of humans, if they do come close to the house then the message from Otherworld is an important one – especially if they leave a feather for us to find. Also magpie feathers can be utilised in spells designed to attract the sort of energy magpies are known for: curiosity, trickery, thievery, gregariousness, creativity and communication. I use magpies to sound the alarm when 'danger' threatens – just as the Iceni took notice of their warning that wolves were about; the bird's services were suitably honoured by a tribute of heather laid near their nest each year.

The most striking thing about a **Jackdaw** is its piercing blue eyes. The irises of adults are greyish or silvery white while those of juveniles are light blue, becoming brownish before whitening at around one year of age. Highly gregarious and noisy, jackdaws are generally seen in flocks of varying sizes, though males and females pair-bond for life and pairs stay together within flocks.

Jackdaws are extremely vocal birds and the main call, frequently given in flight, is a metallic and squeaky *chyak-chyak* or *kak-kak*, which is a contact or greeting call. Perched birds often chatter together, and before settling for the night, large roosting flocks make a cackling noise. They also have a hoarse, drawn-out alarm call, *arrrrr* or *kaaaarr*, used when warning of predators or when mobbing them. If you can get a word in edgeways, ask your question and gauge the response from the bird's reply. The twelfth-century historian William of Malmesbury records the story of a woman who, upon hearing a jackdaw chattering 'more loudly than usual', grew pale and became fearful of suffering a 'dreadful calamity', and that 'while yet speaking, the messenger of her misfortunes arrived'.

And who can deny the thrill of excitement in witnessing that flash of electric blue when an elusive **Jay** flies through the oak or beech wood like some Faere fighter pilot on acid, cackling insanely as it vanished into the undergrowth? The name is believed to come from the Latin word *Gaea*, for Mother Earth, but it has surprisingly few references in folklore and mythology, in spite of its range across the entire Eurasian continents. These birds, like most corvids, are talented mimics, a talent they share with the mynahs and starlings and many parrot species; there has even been a recording of one imitating a house cat! The jay is a wary bird and its harsh, explosive call – a shrill raucous cry repeated two or three times – can be used for divinatory purposes.

Last but certainly not least is the **Chough** that is generally restricted to coastal cliffs and mountains in the far west, although it has now vanished from its traditional Cornish haunts.

The bird has its own fair share of folklore but the most obvious refers to its red legs that associated it with witchcraft because witches were said to wear red stockings for identification. Although, as Stefan Buczacki wryly observes, why they should wish to advertise their wickedness in such a way is not recorded!

An important bird in traditional witchcraft is the **Owl,** and the cry from this bird following the performance of a magical ritual signifies that the message had gone home and been acknowledged. In the Ancient World, the Greeks associated the bird with the goddess Athene and wisdom; and Shakespeare mentions the owl over twenty times, adding to its mystery which is matched by few other birds. Superstition often associated the owl with death, but for the pragmatic Welsh an owl calling continuously around the village merely meant that a local girl was about to lose her virginity. In some areas owls were said to be witches in disguise, but all in all, I would consider an owl to be heralding good fortune rather than bad.

Augury

As we know, the ancient Romans attached considerable importance to the *auguria* or *auspicia*, the object being to determine whether the gods approved or disapproved of some proposed course of action. There were two kinds of omens: those that were deliberately waited and watched for, and those which occurred casually. Omens of the first kind were taken more seriously and alone had legal validity – these included the flight and cries of birds and the behaviour of the sacred chickens. With the passage of time the number of happenings (known as *dirae*) grew so unwieldy that the augers were obliged to close the list!

According to the occult encyclopaedia, *Man, Myth & Magic*, if the omens were to be taken from wild birds, the auger stood on high ground facing east; the area of observation (the *templum*) being marked out in the sky with his curved rod (the *lituus*). He then covered his head and sacrificed to the gods. Not all birds counted for the purpose of augury: those which did were divided into those whose flight was significant (including the eagle, buzzard and vulture) and those whose cries were regarded as ominous (the crow, raven and owl). The woodpecker and osprey belonged to both categories.

The augur (aided by an assistant) had to mark the direction of the flight in relation to the four sections into which the *templum* was divided, the height of the birds above the ground, the rapidity and sound of wing-beats, the frequency, pitch and strength of cries, and their general behaviour. The rules were very complicated and in time a whole technical literature grew up on the subject, which had a jargon of its own. The college of augurs kept archives recording actual cases, and these were used as the basis of handbooks, which explained, for example, that the cry of the crow was a favourable omen if it was heard on the augur's left; that of the raven, if it was heard on the right. They set out the precise meaning of a bird seen shedding its feathers or letting droppings fall.

In Imperial times the art of augury gradually fell out of use, partly because the rules of divination had become so complicated, and the conditions required for favourable omens so numerous, that it became almost impossible to conduct an augury which led to a favourable result! Nevertheless, it is possible to detect remnants of the practice in fractions of our folklore that have come down to the present day.

Augury concerning the prophetic chickens also had its own brand of skullduggery in that the most favourable sign was when the birds ate hungrily, letting food drop from their beaks. Cicero, whose work *On Divination* is the chief ancient source of our knowledge of augury, exposed the practice of keeping the birds in cages and deliberately starved, so that their greediness could not be considered a sign from the gods. Strangely enough, taking the auspices from chickens was a favourite method with Roman generals!

When it comes to divination by birds, however, one of the most spectacular images is the daily roosting display of **Starlings** against the colourful skies of autumn in the cities and the countryside. Until the latter part of the nineteenth century starlings were not common in the British Isles, but their numbers have increased and they are now amongst the most numerous of our resident species. This is confirmed by the number of birds that gather together to form a murmuration.

Thousands of birds flying together in a whirling, ever-changing pattern are a phenomenon of nature that amazes and delights those lucky enough to witness it. As they fly, the starlings in the flock seem to be connected together twisting and turning and changing direction at a moment's notice. The mystery of the murmuration is a fascinating example of a natural phenomenon that hides secrets about the world that scientists have still yet to uncover! But it's one that the witch can tap into and use for divination, asking the question for the birds to answer by creating an enormous image against the setting sun. Focus your mind on the flock and allow yourself to be swept along with its ever-changing movement until you feel the moment is right to mentally phrase the question you need answering ... and see what happens.

Like swans, **Herons** were once royal birds; they are huge birds and magnificent in flight since they cannot be mistaken for anything else. The most widespread and varied of heron lore relates to fishing, but the appearance of a heron and the direction of its flight has always been a favourable sign for me personally. Herons often evaded the hawk by flying into the sun and it was impossible to tell the quarry from its pursuer; if the heron flew away from the sun it was possible to tell a 'hawk from a handsaw' – the latter being a corruption of the old heron name of 'hernshaw'. The heron is also a bird of wisdom and learning, and I always take the time to watch one in its flight.

Magically speaking ...

Feeding the birds is important to the Old Craft witch since these are the creatures of Elemental Air who bring messengers from Otherworld in all sorts of shapes and sizes. On a practical level it provides food at a time when meals are scarce in the wild; and on a spiritual level we are opening up opportunities for channels of communication with our feathered friends. As we have seen, ornithomancy had been practiced by the ancient Greeks, and the Romans developed it as a divinatory method of considerable importance; there are many different techniques. Some observe a bird's flight while others listen to the song; differences in behavioural patterns whether by watching familiar birds or by those sighted in a chance encounter. This type of divination usually falls into two separate forms:

Messages: Whereby the appearance or behaviour of a bird transmits an easily understood instruction often in answer to a current psychic or magical question. In this case the bird is acting as a go-between in conveying a distinct response with some degree of immediacy.

Omens: Also called *portent* or *presage* these phenomena are believed to foretell the future, often signifying the advent of change for good or evil. People in the ancient times believed that omens where a divine message from their gods and therefore required some form of interpretation.

Divination by birds should come automatically for an Old Crafter and while the chattering of the local robin might be delivering a message, the sight of a buzzard – very rare in this part of Ireland – was most definitely an omen and something that required a great deal of thought. This practice is so deeply ingrained that it is part of daily life and as our student observed:

I really understand that *all* is interconnected like a huge spider web and anything on one side, affects something on the other side of the web. I believe animals are completely in tune with that. Animals in our environment help us stay connected to the web of life …

So How Does all this Work?

Importance of Correspondences in Divination

This is the reason why it is essential for all witches to be well versed in nature-lore as well as magical correspondences. It pays to understand the local wildlife otherwise we might not see that unusual 'something' in a bird's normal behaviour patterns.

In *Traditional Witchcraft for Urban Living* I explained that our native flora and fauna are linked to our magical subconscious and we must be receptive to the responses. For those with a working understanding in the language of correspondences, it is easy to grasp how natural the reading of the symbols becomes, and how easy and obvious (in most instances) is the interpretation. For the beginner, however, accept that the answers are not going to appear suddenly like the writing on the wall, foreshowing downfall and disaster at Belshazzar's feast. Divination is more subtle and, more often than not for the inexperienced, irritatingly obtuse!

On a mundane level we need to get used to interpreting the images we receive from our subconscious via our divination techniques. Books will give a basic introduction to the subject of magical correspondences but in reality, interpreting the signs and symbols is more like word association and differ considerably from person to person. Your correspondences will not be mine; both of us may differ from the example given in the books. Let us say, for example, that I've received the impression of an owl in the tea leaves, or crystal ball … or an owl is making its presence felt in the real world.

What does the owl symbolise?

For starters, the bird has been associated with superstitions from just about every culture on the planet … which doesn't help unless we've been working specifically with the Egyptian, Greek or Roman pantheon. But even that doesn't help since we are looking at conflicting interpretations. In ancient Greece, owls were often seen as a symbol of good fortune and associated with the Greek goddess of wisdom, Athene. In contrast, the Romans saw owls as omens of impending disaster. Hearing the hoot of an owl indicated an imminent death, it is thought that the deaths of many famous Romans were predicted by the hoot of an owl, including Julius Caesar, Augustus and Agrippa. While the Greeks believed that sight of an owl predicted victory for their armies, the Romans saw it as a sign of defeat. They believed that a dream of an owl could be an omen of shipwreck for sailors and of being robbed. To ward off the evil caused by an owl, it was believed that the offending owl should be killed and nailed to the door of the affected house. I don't have any particular connection to Greek or Roman deities, so I'm instinctively going to look closer to home – although in a magical context it does pay to have more than a passing interest in the Classics!

Closer to home, in Welsh mythology, Blodeuwedd, the Goddess of Betrayal, is associated with the owl. According to the story in *The Mabinogion*, Blodeuwedd betrayed Llew and the magician Gwydion turned her into a white owl, to haunt the night in loneliness and sorrow, saying: 'I will not slay thee, but I will do unto thee worse than that. For I will turn thee into a bird; and because of the shame thou hast done unto Llew Llaw Gyffes, you shall never show thy face in the light of day. And thou shall not lose thy name, but shall be always called Blodeuwedd.' The word *blodeuwedd* is still used in Wales to mean owl. British folklore also shares a Welsh belief that if an owl is heard amongst houses then an unmarried girl has lost her virginity. And yet another Welsh belief is that if a pregnant woman hears an owl, her child will be blessed. Here I suspect the owl may be warning me of treachery and betrayal from someone close.

What about the bird itself?

Throughout the history of mankind, the owl has featured significantly in mythology and folklore. Owls are one of the few birds that have been found in prehistoric cave paintings and have been both revered and feared throughout many civilisations from ancient to more recent times. In traditional British Old Craft the owl is a sacred bird of the shadows and the giver of wisdom, so I need to think 'outside the box' and try to visualise a situation that puts someone in a position of betrayer. If it's nothing to do with home or family what about career/business?

Is someone trying to out-manoeuvre me on this level? Do I have an undisclosed enemy in the workplace?

What is the bird telling me?

Be alert and watchful. The owl is a silent and deadly hunter that can rip its prey with those sharp talons and beak. Lateral thinking is the secret of a good divination technique.

How do I know if my interpretation is right?

And I'm not off in cloud-cuckoo-land with my imagination running riot? This is where we interact with Nature and look for the signs. If we're roaming the countryside we might find an owl's feather or signs that it's been hunting the night before. Alternatively, we may encounter the image of an owl in an advertisement in a magazine, or a nature programme on television that features an owl. So, having received confirmation that our process of elimination is correct, we can ascertain where the possible threat is coming from in the physical world and be on our guard.

Bird calls and songs constitute a language of signals that although limited is efficient. A widespread belief, common in folk tales, is that under certain circumstance humans can understand the 'speech' of birds, or that birds can understand human language. Folklore also tells of occasional humans born with this gift but more often it is attributed to the imbibing of some herbal or magical concoction. The concept of the bird that brings news can be likened to Odin's two ravens that rove around the world to observe events and gather news; they return to perch on his shoulders and whisper what they have learned in his ear.

Birds regarded as messengers of higher powers or as possessors of secret knowledge have been credited with all manner of remarkable gifts. The annual appearances and disappearances of birds have long aroused mystification and their return in the spring inspired rejoicing (i.e. the swallow and the cuckoo) and in more recent years, letters to *The Times*. In ancient times, however, birds were thought of not merely as heralding the spring but, in a practical sense as being emissaries of the gods, as bringing it. The disappearance of birds in the autumn aroused speculation and disquiet since it was believed that some birds visited the land of the dead. Swallows were thought to disappear beneath the waters of mountain lakes until they re-emerged in the spring – while the folklore of many birds has been determined or influenced by their colouring.

A good deal of oral folklore concerning birds is the residue of more serious beliefs that have disintegrated and decayed over the years as people migrated from the country to the towns. *Man, Myth & Magic* cites the example that:

> The belief that the call of the green woodpecker forecasts rain, is an isolated scrap of information practically devoid of significance until viewed in the context of the ancient beliefs and rituals of which it is the last evidence surviving in the countryside.

The idea of magical correspondences is part of one of the basic beliefs underlying European magic, the conviction that the Universe is not a disorderly collection of stray bits and pieces but an ordered whole, design or pattern. The main strands in the pattern are the correspondences. They are the magical equivalent of a scientist's classification of the phenomena he collects into orderly groups; and they go back to early man's attempts to make sense of his world by classifying things in terms of the gods who controlled them. Our old friend *Man, Myth & Magic* explains:

> The modern magician has substituted for the gods the mysterious currents or forces at work, both in himself and in the universe outside him, but many of the correspondences are drawn from the ancient world and are based, not on any principles known to science but on a symbolic or poetic logic which links together things that outwardly and rationally do not appear to be connected … The dove and the sparrow, for instance, are still said to correspond to Venus, the force of love, just as they were sacred to Aphrodite in Greece, because they are noticeably amorous birds … the cockerel heralds the

dawn and corresponds to the Sun, together with the sparrow-hawk because it soars towards the Sun.

Although the 'system of correspondences' is usually associated with ritual magic, modern witchcraft often utilises the associations without admitting where they come from.

Exercise:

An Appeal for Justice: Divining Guilt or Innocence
[From *The Atum-Re Revival: Ancient Egyptian Wisdom for the Modern World*]

Egyptian law was based on the concept of *ma'at* – the common sense view of right and wrong as defined by the social norms of the day. During the early period of history, *ma'at* was an abstraction represented by the hieroglyph for an ostrich feather. The white ostrich feather suggesting the idea of lightness, and was the only possible comparison that a pure and guiltless heart should have in facing judgement after death. In religious or magical observance, the feather is the perfect offering since it represents the honest and personal integrity of the person performing the ritual as well as being the symbol of the goddess by which we swear. This ritual can be adapted by being addressed to the appropriate dispenser of justice according to your own Path or Tradition and the feather of a bird from your own locality.

The following is an appeal to the goddess for justice for which you will need a soft, curled breast feather, a small square of white paper, four white candles, an appropriate incense and, if possible, a white linen robe. Your Circle should be free of all other adornment with the white candles marking the four quarters. On the square of paper write the cause for requesting judgement and/or the name of the offender. This is particularly appropriate if you suspect you're under psychic attack or ill-wishing, but you're not 100% sure of the sender. Cast your Circle and, sitting on your heels in the centre, hold your hands out with the paper cupped lightly in the palm of your right hand and the feather in your left. Invoke the appropriate goddess, saying:

Lady Ma'at [or Name], Goddess of Truth and Justice
Balance me in harmony that I might
Know and hear my own true self

State your case clearly and concisely. Ask that you be given a sign and if there is a case to be found against your enemy; then request that his/her malice/evildoing be returned to them in accordance with the law of balance and harmony. This method allows for retribution without any excessive use of spite on the petitioner's behalf when you conclude by saying:

I ask for justice to be done according to thy wisdom.

Open your hands and if the feather is blown from your palm it means that the message has been received loud and clear. If, on the other hand, the paper blows from your palm, it may mean that you're blaming the wrong person; that your request is unreasonable; or that you need to re-examine the case again.

Chapter Five

The World of Wyrd

As we've noted before, according to the encyclopaedia, *Man, Myth & Magic*, divination is the prediction of future events or the discovery of secret matters by a great variety of means, signs and occult techniques:

> It is primarily concerned with the future but it sometimes necessitates a turning backwards of the vision in order to learn from the forgotten past. Divination is a gift from the divine: from God or from the gods. This is an intuitive gift, the psychologists say; a magical gift, according to the witch; and an occult one with its own rationale, according to those who have been intimated into the mysteries.

And in its own way, it is all of these things since the Craft does not teach us how to study phenomena, it simply points the way which the seeker is to follow.

Nearly every 'animal, vegetable or mineral', in some part of the world and in all sorts of different cultures has a superstition or folklore attached to it that deems it lucky or unlucky, and its appearance foretells of some future happening. In a round-about-way, divination is linked with what many would call the Fate of an individual; but paradoxically it also echoes what Galadriel says about her mirror in *The Lord of the Rings*:

> *Remember it shows things that were, and things that are, and things that yet may be ... the Mirror shows many things, and not all have yet come to pass. Some may never come to be, unless those that behold the visions turn aside from their path to prevent them...*

A fictional scenario, but it reminds us that it may be our destiny or fate to follow a certain path, the gift we receive in return (i.e. divination) enables us to foresee what lies ahead and if necessary take the necessary measures to prevent those events from happening. There is no scientific explanation, no secrets revealed; just simple ethical 'commandments', the foundation of all magical progress.

The world of Wyrd is a concept in Anglo-Saxon culture roughly corresponding to fate or personal destiny, which is linked to the web of cause-and-effect that permeates the universe. This is not to be viewed as an externally controlling 'fate' but rather as the natural consequences of our own actions; in other words, each person shapes their own destiny. Wyrd therefore does not control our lives, it just responds to our own actions according to the fundamental laws that govern the workings of our world. And if we condense this philosophy into the thought that WWII came into being, not because 'one man had the courage to be evil, but that millions had not the courage to be good' (John Fowles, *The Magus*), we can see how Wyrd can effectively envelope a whole nation.

One of the key concepts of the worldview of the pre-Christian Norse and other Germanic peoples was their unique view of destiny. All beings that are subject to destiny have some degree of power over their own destiny and the destiny of others. Some, however, take this process into their own hands; discerning and shaping destiny is the central concern of heathen Germanic magic. Destiny carved by the Norns is not final and unalterable, as in the Greek concept of fate.

In Old English *wyrd* is a noun formed from *weorþan*, meaning 'to come to pass, to become', although by the fifteenth century, it had developed into 'having the power to control fate' in the form of the origin *Weird Sisters*, i.e. the classical Fates, in the Elizabethan period detached from their classical background as '*fays*', and most notably appearing as the three witches in

Shakespeare's *Macbeth*. In many editions of the play, the editors often include a footnote associating the 'weird sisters' with Old English *wyrd* or 'fate'. And in all honesty, Macbeth's witches were only divining his blood-stained future *if* that was the road *he* chose to go down. Nobody forced him. Had he gone home and remained a loyal subject, packing his wife off to a 'health spa' and keeping the faith with his best mate, he would probably have had a long and very prosperous life!

Divination, whether by 'rod, fingers or birds' or by any other of the hundreds of different methods of 'seeing' helps us keep our foot on the brake, our eye to the future, our finger on the pulse, and our brain in gear. I doubt that a large number of us wouldn't keep on making the same old mistakes if we seriously consulted the crystal ball ... or Tarot ... I-Ching ... at the outset instead of taking target practice to get better at shooting ourselves in the foot!

We're all capable of making the same mistakes over and over when it comes to relationships, money, holidays, career – Freud called this need to repeat a familiar experience despite the unpleasant consequences 'the repetition compulsion'. He believed it was caused by a drive that was both physical and psychological in nature. The truth is that we humans are creatures of habit. We like routines and familiar behaviours, even when they disrupt and distress us. So we repeat them. The psychological part, we have come to understand, may be a desire to master difficult situations. If we do it again and again, our psyche thinks, one time we'll figure out how to make a painful or unpleasant occurrence go differently.

Our behaviour, however, is often dictated by neurons which our brains fire off and those neurons like familiar pathways as much as our psyches and emotions do! Discovering a new approach requires more conscious effort on our part and we also need to remember that even a tiny change often feels uncomfortable at first. The most important point of all is to remember that to change the path which the neurons fire down often means to understand why you want to be different. Most of us want to stay the same, but to have things in our lives change.

A neuron is an electrically excitable cell that processes and transmits information through electrical and chemical signals. Sensory neurons respond to stimuli such as touch, sound or light and all other stimuli affecting the cells of the sensory organs that then send signals to the spinal cord and brain. But to really make a change in your life, you're going to have to slowly retrain those neurons, and knowing why you want them to behave differently can help. *You can't change anything but yourself, but in changing yourself, everything changes around you,* and what initially felt new and awkward soon becomes familiar, comfortable and powerful.

One of the first things a newcomer to Craft is taught is to recognise and accept the existence of 'witch-power', which is the energy we draw on to power our magical applications. Via a series of simple exercises, they begin to realise that this is something tangible that can be physically moved around and controlled – it is not a figment of their imagination. In more simplistic terms, 'witch-power' is similar to the energy raised by *tai chi* – and *tai chi* is widely used within art and sport without any magical significance whatsoever.

The concept of a life force is found in most of the ancient cultures of the world. In India, it is called *prana*; in China, *chi*; in Japan, *ki*; for native Americans, it is the Great Spirit called *Wakan Tanka* among the Sioux, and *Gitche Manitou* in Algonquian. For all these cultures and many others as well, the idea of life force is or was central to their forms of magic, medicine and healing. *Ki* energy is the unseen life force in your body and everywhere. It is a universal energy that penetrates everywhere uniting all the manifestations of the universe, visible or invisible.

It is a perfectly natural energy or force that can be harnessed or tapped into on a daily basis to a greater or lesser extent. A true witch can generate the magical powers necessary by channelling this natural energy from the natural world – in its widest possible sense. And this is what becomes enhanced when we develop the arte of 'seeing' – and get those sensory neurons firing on a different level altogether!

Back to Basics

As David Conway comments wryly in *The Complete Magic Primer*, many people suppose that being a magician (or witch) turns you into something of a soothsayer as well.

This can be embarrassing, especially when friends who know of your occult interests start passing you their dirty teacups in the hope that you can discern their destiny among the slops. People, often perfect strangers, will come up to you at parties, and having announced that they are Aquarians, Virgoans or what have you, will calmly await your analysis of their character and matrimonial prospects.

What separates book-based divination from natural ability is the former's lack of reliance on images coming through from the subconscious, which often knock the preconceived published meanings out of kilter. Hence, the personal Tarot card will always trump those meanings given in the accompanying reader's handbook. As stated earlier, divination is not magic, or spirit messaging, but we can utilise our magical training to access the subconscious which is a universal depositary for all manner of esoteric flotsam and jetsam – and information.

When preparing for a divinatory rite it is advisable to frame a particular question about whatever aspect of the future concerns us *before* the start of the proceedings. Following the casting of lots, or the spread of the cards, in keeping with the ambience of the sacred space we allow a few moments of complete silence to allow our different levels of consciousness to coalesce. Divination is not a magical take-away that provides instant results, it is nothing less than the conscious mind's 'invitation' to the subconscious to take over in order to probe the wealth of information contains in its vaults.

The answer will be forthcoming as a 'received' reading or later in the form of a dream. At no time should we attempt to force an answer since generally these glimpses of the future are quite involuntary and the conscious mind is all too ready to indulge in a flight of fantasy of its own in order to encourage our imagination to take over from the reality. It is better to forget all about the matter until the time comes for the answer to manifest, and often – irritatingly – in allegorical terms, from the subconscious levels of the mind.

When relying on birds (or any other living creature) to predict the future, once we have made a thorough study of their habits in order to detect any unusual behaviour, we can begin to observe things around us in order to detect their relationship to future events. Or to quote again from David Conway:

To sum up, therefore. There are two methods of looking into the future: the first is intuitive, and proceeds from the subconscious to the conscious mind; the second depends on the activity of the conscious mind, and is the process of induction from given data. In most cases, however, there is a little of each ... The adept with prophetic abilities must decide, therefore by which of the many methods available he is going to realise them. He should strive to understand both what he is doing and why he does it, so that all levels of his mind co-operate fully to discover what nature chooses to conceal. Who knows, he may end up as the success of every party he goes to!

If we accept there is always a fundamental reason why certain results are obtained during the divinatory process, it doesn't make it all the less magical. For example, the following extract from a 1935 edition of *The Book of Fortune Telling* describes the use of a traditional 'crystal ball' and I think it is the best no-nonsense view of the subject ever published since it explains why, when the subconscious is given free rein to travel in absolute time, the images observed are actually 'seen' inside the crystal. This 'dislocation' of the subconscious is the secret of crystal-gazing , where the seer suspends all conscious mental activity – having first determined the question to be answered – by fixing the attention to the exclusion of all else on the crystal ball.

The fortune-teller's crystal ball has been around for a long time. In the fifth century, a guild of crystal gazers, known as the *Specularii* was established in Ireland; but the best authorities appear to agree that the practice has its origins in Persia. In an early journal of occultism, *Borderland,* it divided the crystal vision into three separate manifestations:

- Images of things unconsciously observed;
- Images of ideas unconsciously acquired from others;
- Images clairvoyant or prophetic.

Clear rock crystal is the prime material for making crystal balls, but sometimes they are formed from crystal that has been penetrated by numerous inclusions of rutile: long, narrow, needle-like crystals of black or white colouration. The effect is that of needles and thread frozen into a ball of ice. For most crystal gazers such a stone would offer nothing but difficulties, as the object is generally to concentrate on the points of light reflected from the sphere. Continued for any length of time, that procedure will gradually induce a state of self-hypnosis, and then the act of crystal-gazing can properly begin. Many accounts state that the gazer suddenly finds that the globe has disappeared, and has been replaced by a veil of mist upon which visions come and go.

If you are fortunate enough to acquire a crystal (or glass) ball, here are a few good, old-fashioned tips to help you get started:

- The crystal should never be handled by anyone but its owner;
- A black silk handkerchief should be folded round the crystal to exclude reflections;
- Frequent passes made with the right hand gives power to the crystal, and those made with the left hand give it sensitivity which, when the eyes of the gazer look into it, becomes a medium;
- Clouds that appear in the crystal are good omens if they are white, violet, green or blue, but inauspicious if black, red or yellow;
- Ascending clouds answer any question in the affirmative; descending clouds answer in the negative;
- Appearances in the right side of the crystal are of mundane earthly origin; those on the left are symbolic or spiritual images.

Many of the rules laid down by early writers are still essential to success when it comes to crystal gazing and the above are just a few to get you started. There are, however, other aspects to be taken into account and that is that the constant gazing into the crystal eventually causes a form of paralysis of the optic nerve. In *The Curious Lore of Precious Stones*, the celebrated gemmologist George Frederick Kunz explained the phenomena:

The points of light reflected from the polished surface serve to attract the attention of the gazer and to fix the eye until, gradually, the optic nerve becomes so fatigued that it finally ceases to transmit to the sensorium the impression made from without and begin to respond to the reflex action proceeding from the brain of the gazer. In this way the impression received from within is apparently projected and seems to come from without. It is easy to understand that the results must vary according to the idiosyncrasy of the various scryers; for everything depends on the sensitiveness of the optic nerve.

In many cases the effect of prolonged gazing upon the brilliant surface will simply produce a loss of sight, the optic nerve will be temporarily paralysed and will as little respond to stimulation from within as from without; in other cases, however, the nerve will only be deadened as regards external impressions, while retaining sufficient activity to react against a stimulus from the brain centres. It is almost invariably stated that, prior to the appearance of the desired visions, the crystal seems to disappear and a mist rises before the gazer's eyes.

With divination, as with any other form of magical practice, we need to fully understand why we get the results that we do – and it invariably leads to the influence of the subconscious mind. Those involuntary flashes of insight we receive (that usually convinced us of our hidden occult powers in our youth) are merely brief peeks beyond the veil; but if we wish to learn how to make that contact at Will, then we must also accept that the Path will be long, hard, steep and hazardous before we manage to achieve even a partial glimpse of the light beyond.

And so to begin ...

I stated at the beginning of this book that my abilities when it comes to divination have always been limited, but it has not been for the want of trying. I regularly use Crowley's Thoth Tarot and the pendulum for personal divinatory purposes – and with a great deal of success – but tend to rely more on the messages from the natural world like reading a daily copy of the *Telegraph*.

Many witches and pagans of my acquaintance, however, blithely flit from cards to crystals, from candles to corvids but fail to perfect their techniques at reading any in depth. The reason is often a lack of application and the limited time spent in finding the correct method to suit their personality and character. The **Tarot** appears to be the weapon of choice for most witches but how many, truthfully, would *rely* on it when confronted with making a difficult decision in their lives? It may only be that they have tried working with the wrong design or symbolism. I, for instance, could no more read one of those soppy, airy-fairy decks than fly because it would mean nothing to me, but the Thoth Tarot has always spoken to me like an old friend – and never let me down in all the years I've used it.

Again, as an example, I will return to Adrien, who admits to having experiment for years with non-Marseilles-based decks in order to expand his views and learn about correspondences within the different decks until he finally came to the conclusion that he didn't *need* to look elsewhere. He'd bought his first Marseilles deck with pocket money when he was a kid and it has obviously spoken to him like no other.

There are now hundreds of different designs from which to make a selection but take your time and find the one that symbolises *your* kind of magic or belief, and not because it's a series of pretty pictures. The Tarot is also a useful tool for meditation and so it makes sense to find the right deck that links with your subconscious. Start by familiarising yourself with the cards from the Major Arcana that are all based on the archetypal figures from the ancient world and learn the correspondences relating to each card. Try the Celtic Cross spread given above as a *weekly* exercise and try to understand what your cards are telling you, because a prolonged study of the cards can release the diviner's subconscious in just the same way as described for the crystal ball. Then do the same for the Minor Arcana so that you can find your way around the Tarot without resorting to the manufacturer's handbook.

Crystal 'thrall' is a common affliction for newcomers to the pagan scene, simply because they are beautiful to look at but we need to learn more about them before we start an expensive collection that could eventually take over the house. As I've already mentioned previously, I have the most amazing crystal ball collection but generally use them for meditational work by holding the appropriate sphere in the palm of the hand – one for each *sephiroth* of the Qabalah – rather than prediction. Our coven has a strong affinity with the lore of 'stones' because one of our Coven's founders held a doctorate in geology and it became an important subject within the magical teaching.

There are suppliers selling glass 'crystal balls' and crystal spheres made from ground and reconstituted material but the only real issue here is the cost. Undoubtedly we can all envy the personal pleasure of owning a large clear quartz crystal sphere but few of us can afford the luxury of such a beast when a plain glass one will be just as effective when it comes to divination. The important factor is the pinpoints of light that are reflected in the crystal on which we focus our gaze and clear glass will work just as well.

I have three 'balls' that are magically charged. The first is a small clear quartz shot through with rutile that I use solely for meditational work but the second is a huge gold ruby glass the colour of a precious gemstone. The history of the making of this particular type of glass is worthy of note. The first written instructions for making 'gold ruby glass' date back to 1685 when Andreas Cassius published his work, *De Auro,* in which he described for the first time the method of producing a red precipitate of stannic acid with gold, which later became known as the 'Purple of Cassius'. The high price which this glass commanded and the efforts needed to produce it could hardly be justified by its beauty, but the mysticism connected with gold caused the demand. The secret of making red glass was lost for many centuries, and it wasn't rediscovered until the seventeenth century in Bohemia. Johann Kunckel, a chemist from a glass-making family, rediscovered the formula around 1670 and published the results of his experiments in his famous book *Ars Vetraria Experimentalis* in 1679. Today's studio glassmakers can buy their gold ruby glass in rods from specialist manufacturers and although this makes it easier for them, it is still even more expensive. Most gold ruby glass items made today have a thin layer of gold ruby glass coated with clear crystal despite other chemicals producing red glass, none of which have the special magic of gold ruby.

The gold ruby ball cost an absolute fortune, is heavy enough to smash the bones in the toes if dropped on the foot, and is very, very beautiful but it isn't half as effective as the divinatory powers of a plain glass paperweight with a crescent moon cut into it that I procured at an auction of magical paraphernalia I attended with the late Michael Howard back in the 1980s, for the princely sum of £15! A plain glass ' crystal ball' will enable you to get used to the technique but hopefully my story will make you think twice before spending the month's housekeeping on something that is only half as effective as your original old faithful.

Most of our magical rituals are conducted by candlelight and it is not surprising that there are numerous (and effective) divinatory techniques that require the use of a **Candle**. Candle magic is one of the simplest, yet one of the oldest, most powerful forms of spell-casting and divination in any witch's box of tricks, including:

Ceromancy is divination through interpreting the study of the patterns made when molten candle wax is poured into cold water.

Lampadomancy is divination by interpreting visions using the flame of a candle.

Lynchomancy is divination using the wick of a burning candle or lantern to interpret an omen or foretell the future.

Zoanthropy is divination by observing and interpreting the flames of three lighted candles placed in a triangular position.

In Lucya Starza's *Candle Magic* she takes us through the basics and starts by saying that the best way to learn candle prophesy is by doing it – not just reading books:

Divination by candle flame is sometimes called lychnomancy from the Latin '*lychus*' meaning 'light' ...
- A bright, steady flame is considered a good omen.
- If it burns low and dim, the future could be tough.
- One that goes out is bad and indicates some sort of ending.
- A flame that flickers and flutters indicates there are forces acting against you, uncertainty is holding you back, or you might struggle to get what you desire.
- A twisting flame warns you to beware of treachery or unscrupulous people.
- A spark means an important message will be heading your way.
- If a candle burns much more strongly than you expect, is hotter, brighter or burns down extremely fast, you can expect something extraordinary to happen. It might even indicate your wishes will come true in the most unexpectedly good way. Do be careful, because a sudden rise to success can sometimes then be followed by a crash.

Of course, there can be perfectly rational explanations for candles and flames behaving in certain ways. All candles flicker in a wind, burn more slowly in cold weather and burn faster in hot rooms. A wick that is too small for the size of candle will naturally burn with a slow, low flame, while a wick that is too thick for the width of wax will burn extra fast.

So now you've done a simple candle reading you may even be thinking that if it works, why do you need to read a whole book on the subject? Like all aspects of divination there's a simple way and more complex methods that dig deeper into the subconscious and reveal other less obvious signs. For example, a flame burning with different colours is also open to interpretation – the most famous being a blue flame indicating that there is a spirit present in the room as mentioned in Shakespeare's *Richard III*: 'The lights turn blue – it is now dead midnight ...'

Before learning how to divine by birds, we need to find out which of the **Corvids** are plentiful in our location so that we become familiar with them as our neighbours. Carrion crows, magpies and jackdaws are plentiful in urban areas, while hooded crows, rooks, ravens and jays are more common in the countryside. The chough is a rare sighting indeed, since it is a coastal bird from the west but all these are recognised as messengers from Otherworld in Old Craft and we need to be familiar with their body language to determine whether their behaviour is odd, or not. Invest in a book on British birds and begin to study these highly intelligent birds with some degree of seriousness.

Corvids are the witch's equivalent of Western Union and they don't necessarily have to be one of our power (totem) birds which could be from a completely different species. It's also sensible to make sure that your totem bird(s) is something you might encounter in the wild on a fairly regular basis in order to receive any communication or warning that's come your way. After all, we're not going to encounter a penguin or eagle nesting around Chigwell High Street – and the same rules apply to power animals, too!

Divination can be likened to the old joke of the man asking God to help him win the lottery; the request was made on a weekly basis but there was never a result. This routine goes on for weeks with the would-be winner becoming more and more frustrated until finally he yells at the heavens: 'For God's sake help me win the lottery!' And a booming voice responds: 'Can't you meet me half way and buy a ticket!'

If we wish to fully develop our divinatory skills – regardless of the method we choose – then we must be prepared to put in the time and effort into learning everything we can about this particular system. We need to study the background and history, and develop a working knowledge of magical correspondences so that we can work out the vague, the obtuse and the obscure symbolism we 'see' in our readings. Otherwise we can rant and roar at the heavens until we're blue in the face and still not be any closer to achieving our goal of becoming a successful (or even reasonably proficient) diviner.

We have to accept and understand that the Otherworld links between the seer and his divinatory 'tools' are all interconnected like Adrien's huge spider web, and anything on one side, affects something on the other side of the web. Divination links us to the Web of the Wyrd and helps us to discover what the future holds, and to take responsibility for making the right decisions that will affect the rest of our life.

Bibliography

Book of Divining the Future, Eva Shore (Wordsworth)

Cold Reading: Confessions of a 'Psychic', Colin Hunter (interview)

The Curious Lore of Precious Stones, George Frederick Kunz (Dover)

The Complete Magical Primer, David Conway (Aquarian)

A Companion to Greek Studies (4th ed.) E.A. Gardner (1931CUP)

A Demotic Inscribed Icosahedron, Martina Minas-Nerpel (EES *Journal* 2007 Vol.93) *An Encyclopaedia of Occultism,* Lewis Spence (1920 ...)

Fauna Britannica, Stefan Buczacki (Hamlyn)

The History of Magic, Kurt Seligmann (QPBC)

I-Ching in Plain English, George Hulskramer (Souvenir Press)

Liber 777, Aleister Crowley (Weiser)

The Magical Arts, Richard Cavendish (Arkana)

Magic Crystals, Sacred Stones, Melusine Draco (Axis Mundi)

Man, Myth & Magic, ed. Richard Cavendish (Marshall Cavendish)

Pagan Portals: Candle Magic, Lucya Starza (Moon Books)

The Penguin Guide to the Superstitions of Britain and Ireland, Steve Roud (Penguin)

The Power of the Pendulum, T C Lethbridge (Routledge & Kegan Paul)

Root & Brach: British Magical Tree Lore, Melusine Draco (Ignotus)

Traditional Witchcraft For Urban Living, Melusine Draco (Moon Books)

Traditional Witchcraft for Woods and Forests, Melusine Draco (Moon Books)

The Viking Spirit: Norse Mythology and Religion, Dan McCoy (...)

Witchcraft – A Traditional Renewed, Even John Jones (Hale)

The Witching Herbs: 13-Essential Plants and Herbs for Your Magical Garden, Harold Roth (Weiser)

About the Author

Mélusine Draco is an Initiate of traditional British Old Craft and the Khemetic Mysteries. Her highly individualistic teaching methods and writing draw on historical sources supported by academic texts and current archaeological findings; endorsing Crowley's view that magic is an amalgam of science and art, and that magic is the outer route to the inner Mysteries. Author of several titles currently published with John Hunt Publishing including the best-selling six-part Traditional Witchcraft series; two titles on power animals – *Aubry's Dog* and *Black Horse, White Horse; By Spellbook & Candle; By Wolfsbane & Mandrake Root; Pan: Dark Lord of the Forest and Horned God of the Witches; The Dictionary of Magic & Mystery* published by Moon Books; *Magic Crystals Sacred Stones* and *The Atum-Re Revival* published by Axis Mundi Books. Her esoteric novels, *The Temple House Archive* series are available in both paperback and e-book formats – all books are available on Amazon.

Web:
www.covenofthescales.com and www.templeofkhem.com

Blog:
https://wordpress.com/pages/melusine-draco.blog

Melusine Draco on Facebook:
https://www.facebook.com/Melusine-Draco-486677478165958
Facebook: http://www.facebook.com/TradBritOldCraft
Facebook: http:// www.facebook.com/TempleofKhem
Facebook: http://www.facebook.com/TempleHouseArchive
Facebook: http://www.facebook.com/IgnotusPressUK

We think you will also enjoy...

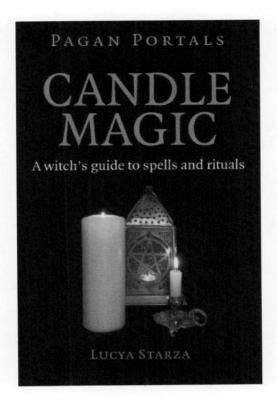

Candle Magic, Lucya Starza

Using candles in simple spells, seasonal rituals and essential craft techniques.

...a comprehensive guide on how to use candles for spells, in rituals and for meditation and divination. It has quickly become my preferred book for all aspects of candle magic.
Philip Heselton

978-1-78535-043-6 (Paperback)
978-1-78535-044-3 (e-book)

Celtic Chakras, Elen Sentier

Tread the British native shaman's path, explore the Goddess
hidden in the ancient stories; walk the Celtic chakra spiral
labyrinth.

Rich with personal vision, the book is an interesting exploration of
wholeness
Emma Restall Orr

978-1-78099-506-9 (paperback)
978-1-78099-507-6 (e-book)

Best Selling Pagan Portals & Shaman Pathways

Druid Shaman, Danu Forest

A practical guide to Celtic shamanism with exercises and techniques as well as traditional lore for exploring the Celtic Otherworld

A sound, practical introduction to a complex and wide-ranging subject
Philip Shallcrass

978-1-78099-615-8 (paperback)
978-1-78099-616-5 (e-book)

Kitchen Witchcraft, Rachel Patterson
Take a glimpse at the workings of a Kitchen Witch and share in
the crafts

*A wonderful little book which will get anyone started on Kitchen
Witchery. Informative, and easy to follow*
Janet Farrar & Gavin Bone

978-1-78099-843-5 (paperback)
978-1-78099-842-8 (e-book)

Best Selling Pagan Portals & Shaman Pathways

Moon Magic, Rachel Patterson
An introduction to working with the phases of the Moon

...a delightful treasury of lore and spiritual musings that should be essential to any planetary magic-worker's reading list.
David Salisbury

978-1-78279-281-9 (paperback)
978-1-78279-282-6 (e-book)

Best Selling Pagan Portals & Shaman Pathways

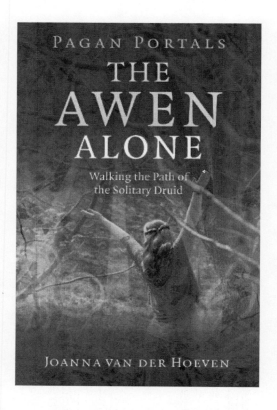

The Awen Alone, Joanna van der Hoeven
An introductory guide for the solitary Druid

Joanna's voice carries the impact and knowledge of the ancestors,
combined with the wisdom of contemporary understanding.
Cat Treadwell

978-1-78279-547-6 (paperback)
978-1-78279-546-9 (e-book)

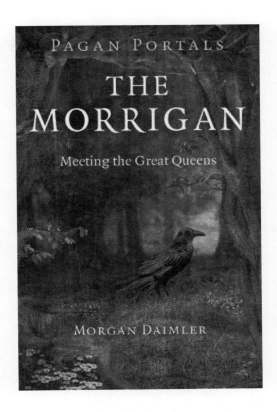

The Morrigan, Morgan Daimler

On shadowed wings and in raven's call, meet the ancient Irish
Goddess of war, battle, prophecy, death, sovereignty, and magic

*...a well-researched and heartfelt guide to the Morrigan from a fellow
devotee and priestess*
Stephanie Woodfield

978-1-78279-833-0 (paperback)
978-1-78279-834-7 (e-book)

MOON

BOOKS

PAGANISM & SHAMANISM

What is Paganism? A religion, a spirituality, an alternative belief system, nature worship? You can find support for all these definitions (and many more) in dictionaries, encyclopaedias, and text books of religion, but subscribe to any one and the truth will evade you. Above all Paganism is a creative pursuit, an encounter with reality, an exploration of meaning and an expression of the soul. Druids, Heathens, Wiccans and others, all contribute their insights and literary riches to the Pagan tradition. Moon Books invites you to begin or to deepen your own encounter, right here, right now.

If you have enjoyed this book, why not tell other readers by posting a review on your preferred book site. Recent bestsellers from Moon Books are:

Journey to the Dark Goddess
How to Return to Your Soul
Jane Meredith
Discover the powerful secrets of the Dark Goddess and transform your depression, grief and pain into healing and integration.
Paperback: 978-1-84694-677-6 ebook: 978-1-78099-223-5

Shamanic Reiki
Expanded Ways of Working with Universal Life Force Energy
Llyn Roberts, Robert Levy
Shamanism and Reiki are each powerful ways of healing; together, their power multiplies. *Shamanic Reiki* introduces techniques to help healers and Reiki practitioners tap ancient healing wisdom.
Paperback: 978-1-84694-037-8 ebook: 978-1-84694-650-9

Pagan Portals – The Awen Alone
Walking the Path of the Solitary Druid
Joanna van der Hoeven
An introductory guide for the solitary Druid, *The Awen Alone* will accompany you as you explore, and seek out your own place within the natural world.
Paperback: 978-1-78279-547-6 ebook: 978-1-78279-546-9

A Kitchen Witch's World of Magical Herbs & Plants
Rachel Patterson
A journey into the magical world of herbs and plants, filled with magical uses, folklore, history and practical magic. By popular writer, blogger and kitchen witch, Tansy Firedragon.
Paperback: 978-1-78279-621-3 ebook: 978-1-78279-620-6

Medicine for the Soul
The Complete Book of Shamanic Healing
Ross Heaven
All you will ever need to know about shamanic healing and how to become your own shaman...
Paperback: 978-1-78099-419-2 ebook: 978-1-78099-420-8

Shaman Pathways – The Druid Shaman
Exploring the Celtic Otherworld
Danu Forest
A practical guide to Celtic shamanism with exercises and
techniques as well as traditional lore for exploring the Celtic
Otherworld.
Paperback: 978-1-78099-615-8 ebook: 978-1-78099-616-5

Traditional Witchcraft for the Woods and Forests
A Witch's Guide to the Woodland with Guided Meditations and
Pathworking
Melusine Draco
A Witch's guide to walking alone in the woods, with guided
meditations and pathworking.
Paperback: 978-1-84694-803-9 ebook: 978-1-84694-804-6

Wild Earth, Wild Soul
A Manual for an Ecstatic Culture
Bill Pfeiffer
Imagine a nature-based culture so alive and so connected,
spreading like wildfire. This book is the first flame...
Paperback: 978-1-78099-187-0 ebook: 978-1-78099-188-7

Naming the Goddess
Trevor Greenfield
Naming the Goddess is written by over eighty adherents and
scholars of Goddess and Goddess Spirituality.
Paperback: 978-1-78279-476-9 ebook: 978-1-78279-475-2

Shapeshifting into Higher Consciousness
Heal and Transform Yourself and Our World with Ancient
Shamanic and Modern Methods
Llyn Roberts
Ancient and modern methods that you can use every day to
transform yourself and make a positive difference in the world.
Paperback: 978-1-84694-843-5 ebook: 978-1-84694-844-2

Readers of ebooks can buy or view any of these bestsellers by
clicking on the live link in the title. Most titles are published in
paperback and as an ebook. Paperbacks are available in traditional
bookshops. Both print and ebook formats are available online.

Find more titles and sign up to our readers' newsletter at
http://www.johnhuntpublishing.com/paganism
Follow us on Facebook at https://www.facebook.com/MoonBooks
and Twitter at https://twitter.com/MoonBooksJHP